Cornwall
First World War

Pete London

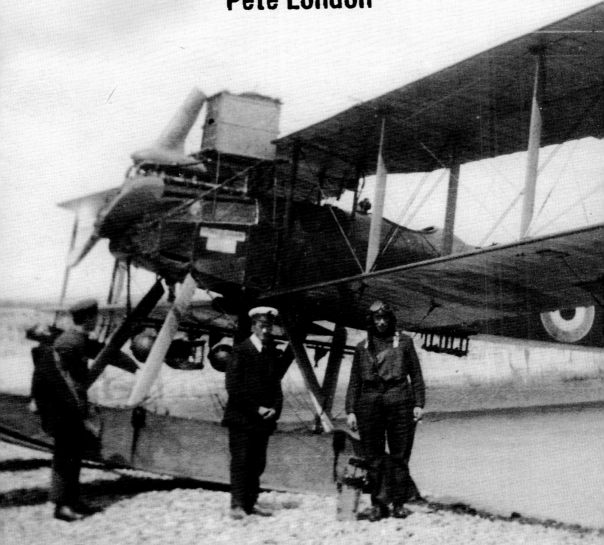

First published 2013

Published by Truran

Truran is an imprint of Tor Mark, United Downs Ind. Est., St Day, Redruth TR16 5HY

ISBN 978 185022 244 6

Designed by Alix Wood www.alixwood.co.uk

Printed by Hedgerow Print, 16 Marsh Lane, Lords Meadow Industrial Estate, Crediton, Devon EX17 1ES

Cornwall in the First World War

Contents

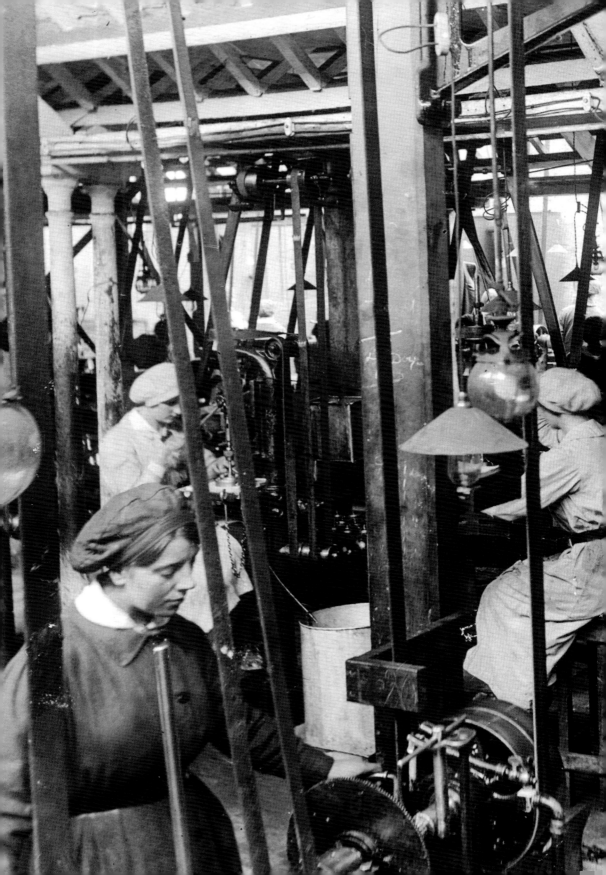

Chapter 1 - Outbreak

Prelude

Jᴜʟʏ 1914: Bʀɪᴛᴀɪɴ's holiday season was sultry, harvests full of promise. In towns and cities, crowds of excited trippers boarded railways bound for the warm seaside. As their trains meandered through green and yellow country, children watched farm hands labouring in fields, horses at work or nibbling the stubble. Soon, most of the animals and men would be gone.

That month too, off the south coast between Spithead and the Isle of Wight, the Royal Navy's mighty fleets gathered for the pageant of review by King George V. Dozens of vessels anchored in lines stretching for miles, their cold grey iron a sledgehammer show of imperial strength: towering battleships, cruiser squadrons, shoals of destroyers. Britain's global dominion was impregnable, her realm supreme.

Until recently, reports of trouble in the Balkans had worried few people. Now and then, newspapers touched on obscure little conflicts between the region's humble states. But the major powers of Austria-Hungary and Russia took a closer interest in south-east Europe, both seeking to strengthen their influence there.

Serbia was a recent bone of contention, a small nation shakily-independent but coveted by both empires. Austria had already annexed the former Serbian provinces of Bosnia and Herzegovina. When the heir to Austria's throne, Archduke Franz Ferdinand, was assassinated in Bosnia's capital Sarajevo during a visit in June 1914, Austria accused Serbia of backing their fellow-Slavs' nationalism by concocting the plot.

Austrian anger was followed by belligerent demands of Serbia, really an ultimatum amounting to control over the country's affairs. Serbia's response was appeasing but finally, pretence at negotiation waived, on 28 July Austria declared war. Power in the Balkans would be resolved once and for all, by force. But the treaties, tensions and enmities between Europe's most dominant nations ensured Austria couldn't act in a vacuum.

On the international stage, threats and brinkmanship spiralled. Deeply troubled by Russia's recent rearmament programme, and viewing the Serbian crisis as an excuse to attack first if needs be, Germany promised support for Austria. Russia, in turn, was bound by treaty to Serbia; Tsar Nicholas I put his armies on a war-footing.

▲ Overlooking Mount's Bay, fleets of war and peace share the great harbour. The Royal Navy made numerous calls before the fighting, while Newlyn's fishing boats went about their usual business (AUTHOR'S COLLECTION).

The French, who'd signed a treaty with Russia and Britain, began to muster their forces; so did Britain. On 1 August Germany, seeing the Tsar's mobilisation of his troops as an act of war against Austria, declared war on Russia. Two days later, on a long-planned second front Germany struck at France through neutral Belgium, whose security Britain had guaranteed; by 4 August Britain and Germany were at war.

No-one stayed untouched. The First World War affected every town and village in Britain while politics, social order and the role of women in society were forever altered. Losses were truly terrible, millions killed or wounded. Afterwards the war's weight lay heavily with many who'd returned, often for a lifetime.

Today, although a century has passed there's still proximity to the events of those four years, sustained by grainy film and faded sepia images reminding us of the fighting. We don't have to look too far back to find those who joined up, whether frock-coated, flat-capped or long-skirted. And Cornwall's part in the great confrontation would be vital.

Mobilisation

A S NEWSPAPERS GREAT and small conveyed the unfolding events that summer, outbreak of war was marked by funeral-black headlines. In Penzance, the *Cornishman* led with: 'Europe at War: Dreadful and Incredible Nightmare is a Reality'. The *Royal Cornwall Gazette* bellowed: 'A Continent in Arms. Great Britain Accepts Germany's Challenge. A Fight for Honour, Truth and Justice'. Liskeard's *Cornish Times* settled for the unadorned 'War with Germany'. In towns and villages across the Duchy patriotic crowds formed, local bands turned out, flags were run up.

Tywardreath woman Mrs George later recalled the first warning of war her father had received was the sound of cheering, coming from the direction of the railway station; he telephoned the station-master who told him the news. At Mevagissey's Town Bridge, watching local men gather in a show of nationalism, 3-year-old Mary Lakeman clung to her tearful mother's hand. As Britain's small standing army left for France and began its campaign, the papers' jingoism soared; military setbacks were portrayed as cunning preludes to victory, the enemy as barbaric baby-killers.

▲ Before the war, British C Class submarines C.31 and C.32 called at Penzance to fly the Navy's flag. Curiously, they were marked 61 and 62. On the quayside local people admire the new-fangled technology. By October 1917, both craft had been lost (AUTHOR'S COLLECTION).

▲ August 1914: men of the Naval Reserve gather at Redruth's railway station, mobilised and on their way to fight. Around the reservists are women and children, come to see them off (AUTHOR'S COLLECTION).

One of the first to join the fight was the Duke of Cornwall's Light Infantry. Formed during 1881, the regiment had its headquarters at Bodmin's grey stone Victoria Barracks. In August 1914 its 1st Battalion of regulars was serving in Ireland at the Curragh; their reservists, who in peacetime had jobs outside the military, journeyed from far and wide to muster at Bodmin. There they were kitted out with uniforms and equipment before travelling on to assemble in County Kildare. By mid-month 1st Battalion had embarked in the SS *Lanfranc*, bound from Dublin to Le Havre; at dawn on 23 August they encountered their first Germans. That day Private William Thomas Gow became the regiment's opening casualty of the war.

That month too some of the Duchy's dreaded workhouses, usually refuges for destitute people, were put to a new use: custody of aliens. With deeply unlucky timing, just as war came two German liners sailing for America put in at Falmouth. The Hamburg America vessel *Prince Adalbert* (Captain Schonfeldt) arrived on 4 August, closely followed by *Kronprinzessin Cecilie*. Their crews and several hundred passengers were transferred in batches to Custom House Quay by Falmouth's tug *Victor* and detained, some briefly held in stinking quayside fish-houses.

▶ Swamped by his new greatcoat, a young recruit to the Duke of Cornwall's Light Infantry poses for his photograph before leaving for war (AUTHOR'S COLLECTION).

Both vessels were seized by the Admiralty; the aliens, harmless and by no means all Germans (some were Americans), were taken under armed guard to the workhouses at Falmouth, Helston, Penzance, Redruth, St Columb Major and Truro. American citizen Theodore Cuyler Patterson of Philadelphia protested loudly, claiming he was a personal friend of President Wilson; it made no difference. With neutrals finally weeded out though, by the end of September St Columb Major's austere lodgings had received 71 reluctant residents; later they were moved up-country.

▲ Among the Cornishmen who joined up when war broke out was St Austell-born Percival Phillips; later he served with the Royal Flying Corps in Mesopotamia. Here he's in the cockpit of his R.E.8 two-seat biplane. 'PP' returned safely, and post-war formed the Cornwall Aviation Company (AUTHOR'S COLLECTION).

▲ August 1914: aliens from German ships which docked at Falmouth at the time war was declared. Escorted by policemen, they've been marched up Redruth's West End hill on their way to detention at Barncoose workhouse. Local children walk alongside (AUTHOR'S COLLECTION).

▲ Territorial soldiers from Padstow assemble at a makeshift camp before leaving for the front. They're certainly a piratical-looking crew (MALCOLM McCARTHY COLLECTION).

By contrast, the previous month an enemy departure had taken place. Austria's Ambassador to Britain, Count Albert von Mensdorff, was expelled; he left the country via Falmouth, bound for Genoa aboard the SS *Aaro*. During September more German ships arrived in the great port: four-masted barque *Goldbeck* carrying wheat, captured by a British cruiser off the Lizard; the *Orlando*, taken with a cargo of Chilean nitrate used in making high explosives; schooner *Caracas*; and Teutonically-named *Fritz*, also with nitrate.

That autumn the DCLI expanded; with astonishing haste several New Army battalions took shape, their men joining for the war's duration only. In August and September three battalions formed at Bodmin, a fourth at Falmouth during October. Luckier troops, often the officers, were put up by local people or at hotels and inns for around a shilling (5p) a day. Every available space was used for accommodation: at Falmouth the Drill Hall, the Passmore Edwards Library and the Boy's Brigade barracks were all pressed. For the lower ranks, often it was temporary canvas villages of bell-tents and field kitchens, which sprang up around the towns' outskirts.

▲ 1/5th Battalion DCLI photographed at Place House, St Anthony, on the Roseland. The Battalion moved to Falmouth on mobilisation but by end of August 1914 was at Salisbury Plain (AUTHOR'S COLLECTION).

▲ A column of 3rd Battalion DCLI, assembled and on the march (AUTHOR'S COLLECTION).

In November the 2nd Battalion of DCLI regulars returned to Britain, recalled from Hong Kong, but quickly travelled on to Le Havre. The 3rd (Reserve) Battalion mobilised at Bodmin but for a time moved to Falmouth; they also provided guards at Poldhu on the Lizard for Guglielmo Marconi's wireless station, and at the premises of Cornish explosives manufacturers.

Meanwhile the Regiment's Territorial battalions, part-time soldiers, had been rallying. In August the 1/4th Battalion assembled at Truro, the 1/5th at Bodmin; initially they took up war stations at Falmouth but went to Salisbury Plain for training. Cornwall's railway platforms became crammed, stations packed with eager new volunteers, seasoned troops and reservists on the move. Special trains were laid on to transport the men while people from nearby villages flocked to see them off, cheering and waving flags.

Recruits also joined the colours from Cornwall's most prominent homes, though not all were from the grand families themselves. At Heligan House near Mevagissey, no fewer than 22 of the gardening staff enlisted in the DCLI; by 1916 the 1000-acre estate was tended by just eight men. The castle lads working at Caerhays signed on. Near Bodmin, imposing Lanhydrock House was owned by the Agar-Robartes family; eldest son Tommy volunteered for the Royal Bucks Hussars as a 2nd Lieutenant, later serving with the Coldstream Guards. From Trengwainton House near Penzance, Edward (later Sir Edward) Bolitho joined the Royal Artillery.

But not everyone enlisted in the army; before the war, many Cornish fishermen and coastguards had signed up with the Royal Naval Reserve. From ports all along Cornwall's shores, from August streams of mobilised men left their fleets for naval depots, many travelling initially to Devonport. Pleasure-boats ceased their trips between Falmouth and the Lizard's Church Cove. St Agnes lost every one of its coastguards, all of them reservists. At Mousehole, call-up papers arrived during Sunday worship; the fishermen left in the middle of the service.

For those seafarers who stayed in Cornwall too there would be action aplenty. In 1910 the RNR's Trawler Section had been formed, to recruit and train fishermen for a particular form of naval service. After the outbreak, Germany's widespread sea-mining operations around the British coast led to a huge growth in the work of the RNR. Cornwall's fishing fleets were sharply cut, as dozens of craft were taken over and armed as auxiliary minesweepers. Under prior agreements with the Admiralty the crews sailed their small vessels to naval dockyards to be fitted out with armament, magazines and minesweeping gear.

▲ Padstow Territorials and their sturdy mounts gathering for service during the autumn of 1914 (MALCOLM MCCARTHY COLLECTION).

The Trawler Section mariners played a valuable but costly part in the war at sea, drawing on intimate knowledge of the waters around the Duchy. Their work was dangerous and never-ending: repeatedly, harbours, channels and anchorages had to be swept to ensure vital areas were free of mines. The sailors attended to mine defences at harbour approaches, and later in the war helped provide convoy escorts. The Admiralty also instructed that whenever possible, Cornwall's reduced fisher-fleets be accompanied by armed vessels, themselves often converted trawlers.

Nor was it just men who joined up. The DCLI was an infantry regiment so its use of horses was limited, but the wider peacetime British Army owned thousands of beasts as mounts and for pulling guns and wagons. After the outbreak that wasn't nearly enough, and like other areas Cornwall was scoured for more animals. During August 1914 alone the military took scores of horses; hardly any of them came home.

Along the shoreline facing France, to counter possible German attacks Cornwall's coastal fortifications were hurriedly reinforced. Even Henry VIII's Tudor castles at Pendennis and St Mawes were pressed, equipped with gun batteries to cover the waters around Falmouth. Since Henry's reign Pendennis had been modernised several times, re-armed in the mid- and late-1800s and later fitted with quick-firing guns against the threat of enemy motor torpedo boats.

Below Pendennis, Crab Quay's Edwardian battery received powerful Defence Electric Lights trained out to sea, to seek out out the foe at night. On the Roseland, the Victorian fort at St Anthony's Head was occupied by Cornwall Royal Garrison Artillery troops, its peacetime force buttressed against possible German raids, while more searchlights arrived.

To the east, near Plymouth's huge naval base, several Cornish forts and gun batteries from the Victorian era played a part in the war. Some had appeared during the 1860s, built by order of Prime Minister Viscount Palmerston to deter a supposed threat from France. Largest was Tregantle Fort, completed in 1865 on the Rame peninsula east of Downderry, overlooking Whitsands Bay; it could house 1,000 men and 35 guns. At the bay's eastern end, equipped with seven 64-pounder muzzle-loading guns, Polhawn Battery was commissioned during 1867.

Nearby, Cawsands Battery was set on a rise overlooking the village, its first soldiers arriving in 1863. By the River Lynher, polygonal Scraesdon Fort was completed during 1862, a complicated base originally equipped for 27 7-inch guns; a small railway line

▲ Recruits to the Royal Naval Air Service form up for their group photograph during initial training at Tregantle Fort (AUTHOR'S COLLECTION).

▲ The long low profile of Tregantle. During the First World War the great stronghold was used for training, storage and shooting practice, by the army and later the navy (STEVE JOHNSON/CYBERHERITAGE).

linked it with Tregantle. Picklecombe Fort appeared at the Rame peninsula's easternmost point near Mount Edgcumbe; at first it received 32 10-inch, 9-inch and 7-inch muzzle-loaders, set in an arc of two-storey casemates faced with granite blocks and iron shields. Later, more modern 6-inch breech-loaders and quick-firing weapons arrived. North of Picklecombe was the smaller Garden Battery.

In the 1890s a new generation of shoreline defences had been built. North of Kingsand and intended for a garrison of around 90 men, Hawkins Battery was completed during 1892. By 1914 it had been re-equipped, the old high-angle-fire 9-inch guns replaced by 9.2-inch breech-loaders. Neighbour Raleigh Battery wasn't so lucky; finished in 1894, by 1910 its guns had been removed though it continued to serve as a lowly store.

During their 19th century lives Cornwall's eastern forts had been underused; despite Palmerston's dread, the French never came. After August 1914 though, from early in the war they were employed for musketry training by visiting Regiments, as barracks for new recruits and later for storage of all sorts; at Tregantle, even balloons and aeroplanes were packed down. Picklecombe's two 6-inch breech loaders became an examination battery. Experts disagree over Cawsand's role; some believe its guns had gone before the war.

Just under 30 miles off Land's End at St Mary's, principal of the Isles of Scilly, between 1898 and 1905 several gun batteries had appeared. The batteries added to the existing defensive complex on the south-west headland of St Mary's known as the Garrison, which had its roots in Elizabethan times.

By 1901 two large batteries named Woolpack and Steval were in place, armed with pairs of 6-inch breech-loading guns. Smaller positions were constructed at Steval Point, and Bant's Carn north of Halangy Point, both intended for 12-pounder quick-firing guns to deal with speedy torpedo-boats. During the Edwardian era though, Woolpack and Steval had their guns taken away, while no quick-firers arrived. But soon after August 1914 the island's troops were reinforced, keeping a vigilant watch over beaches and the surrounding seas.

▲ Picklecombe Fort was built between 1861 and 1867. Initially armed with muzzle-loading guns, through the First World War it was manned by soldiers from the Royal Garrison Artillery (AUTHOR'S COLLECTION).

Chapter 2 - Build-Up

The Navy Arrives

FROM THE BEGINNING of the war, Britain's surrounding seas became strategically crucial. The constant flow of merchant ships bringing essential food, raw materials and military equipment had to be given all possible protection; so did vessels supplying the armies in France. For beneath those waters the slow defenceless craft were stalked by Germany's U-boat submarines, let loose in a bitter campaign which grew horrifically successful.

On 22 September 1914, submarine U-9 sank three British cruisers in under an hour; by the end of December 15 ships had been hit. Near the Isles of Scilly, 25 miles off Bishop Rock, on 12 March 1915 U-29 sank three British merchant steamers; that year a total of 755 ships were sent to the bottom. It quickly became obvious determined submarine operations against Britain's sea lanes could fatally weaken her power to fight on.

Cornwall was very soon a vital part of the maritime front-line. True, much of Britain's coast became involved in the war on Germany's U-boats. But it was Cornwall's position at the conjunction of so many mercantile shipping routes vulnerable to the submarines, its craggy profile thrusting into the Channel's western entrance, reaching out to the Celtic Sea and tipping the Atlantic, which made the Duchy so important.

◀ 12 March 1915: off Bishop Rock, German submarine U-29 stalks the British merchant ship SS *Headlands*. The vessel was sunk by a torpedo which struck abaft her engine-room; the crew had taken to lifeboats and were saved (AUTHOR'S COLLECTION).

► From the war's opening shots, naval activity at Falmouth and Penzance intensified. Here, a torpedo boat sets out to patrol the Channel (MALCOLM McCARTHY COLLECTION).

To help oppose the grave threat, the Royal Navy quickly reinforced its Cornish presence. Falmouth was declared a defended harbour, the huge natural port adopted as a headquarters for naval forces west of the Rame Peninsula. The steamer *New Resolute* was posted near St Anthony lighthouse to watch over shipping movements, while minesweepers and armed trawlers kept the harbour's channels safe.

Between Pendennis and St Mawes, even before the war a protective minefield had been laid to deter underwater enemies. Later, anti-submarine nets appeared. As the conflict escalated Falmouth became a major supply depot for Britain's armies across the Channel; merchant shipping, steam and sail, poured in and out. The port's great dry-dock, spread over 120 acres and long used for ship-repair, became saturated with work.

▲ British merchantman SS *Coath* in Mount's Bay. During December 1916 she was torpedoed and sunk by UB-38; 16 crewmen died including her master, Luke Spargo Berryman of Penzance (AUTHOR'S COLLECTION).

In February 1915 the Navy arrived at Penzance. Mount's Bay had long been a favourite anchorage for passing British fleets, and a base was needed west of congested Falmouth. Also, as the U-boats broadened their searches, the outpost allowed a greater area to be patrolled by the Navy's shore-based vessels.

At the heart of Penzance harbour-front, N Holman & Sons' dry dock was requisitioned; over the offices a White Ensign was raised, the base commanded by Lieutenant Commander David Blair, RNR. Like Falmouth, Mount's Bay became home to minesweepers, drifters and armed trawlers. On the north coast at Padstow plans were made to receive more patrol craft, while a westernmost station was created on the Isles of Scilly at St Mary's with a small mixed group of impressed boats.

Deadly Training: HMS *Defiance*

At the mouth of the River Lynher meanwhile, Cornwall's naval station HMS *Defiance* continued its lethal business. Commissioned late in 1884 the base had been formed at Wearde Quay near Saltash, built around two wooden hulks moored off the river's northern bank: *Defiance*, an outmoded 2nd rater launched in 1861 after which the

▲ Wooden walls: HMS *Defiance*, the Victorian hulk around which Cornwall's naval training station was built on the River Lynher (STEVE JOHNSON/CYBERHERITAGE).

▲ On the Lynher, early British submarines A.7 and A.9 lurk alongside the supply vessel carrying their stores and spare torpedoes. In an accident off Whitsand Bay A.7 was lost with all hands; A.9 survived the war (STEVE JOHNSON/CYBERHERITAGE).

station was named, and the smaller sloop *Perseus*. During 1905 a railway line was added, its station named Defiance Halt, connecting the sailors with Great Western's route to the diverse attractions of Plymouth waterfront.

Between them the vessels provided quarters for officers and ratings on main and lower decks respectively, as well as a galley, gymnasium, and also lecture rooms, for *Defiance* was a training station. Its courses taught wholesale maritime destruction, using some of the deadliest weapons of their day: torpedoes and enormous sea-mines.

Defiance operated various craft, including the gunboat *Scourge* fitted with an 18-inch aluminium torpedo tube; a steam pinnace, numerous torpedo boats and a destroyer also served. The main hulk itself was fitted with training torpedo-tubes, pointed toward the mud flats across the river. Using the other vessels live exercises were regularly carried out in Plymouth Sound, a torpedo-range cleared of traffic apart from moored tender HMS *Falcon*, which spotted and marked the students' efforts.

Mine-laying practice and recovery drills, using dummy weapons, were generally performed in Whitsand and Cawsand Bays. But live mine and torpedo firings even took place on the Lynher itself. Along the shore Cornish people would gather to watch the explosions, as colossal gouts of water were flung high into the air.

By 1907 the hulk HMS *Spartan* had joined *Defiance*, serving throughout the First World War. As well as its training role, the base continued work on improving torpedoes, torpedo-launchers and tubes, and all facets of mine warfare, while experimental trials were conducted in its wireless and electrical workshops.

Occasionally Wearde Quay was visited by submarines, including some of Britain's earliest submersibles: the A Class, dating back to 1903. The tiny craft suffered from poor seagoing qualities; on the surface they had miserable freeboard, and would roll in the slightest waves. In January 1914, during practice torpedo attacks in Whitsand Bay against HMS *Onyx* and HMS *Pigmy*, submarine A.7 had failed to surface. The 11 crewmen aboard all perished and A.7 was never recovered. Cornish people had been shocked by the tragedy, and contributed to a public fund set up to help the families left behind. Just before the war two of the later C Class submarines called, travelling on to Penzance where the public viewed them with great interest; by 1917 both had been lost.

▲ Divers at HMS *Defiance* equipped with the bulky, weighty underwater costumes of the day. The seaman to the left wears a massive metal helmet (STEVE JOHNSON/CYBERHERITAGE VIA DEREK TAIT).

Airships

In February 1915 Germany declared a policy of wholesale submarine warfare around the British Isles. All enemy shipping found would be attacked, while neutral vessels entered British waters at their peril. Among the Admiralty's responses to the heightened menace was the creation of numerous coastal airship stations, run by the Royal Naval Air Service. Airships were ideal for long patrols to hunt the U-boats. They could stay aloft for many hours and carry several bombs, while their wireless equipment would assist co-operation with the Navy's ships in pressing home attacks.

▲ Mullion's airship C2 manoeuvres across the station, her ground crew in attendance. Behind are the station's two massive airship sheds, the second under construction. The huge doors of the right-hand shed gape open, and a windbreak is in place to protect the airships from gusts (AUTHOR'S COLLECTION).

One of the areas chosen for an airship base was the Lizard peninsula. A station there would be key in helping defend the Channel, and allow flights westward over the Atlantic. In June 1916 Royal Naval Air Station Mullion opened for business, built on 320 acres of land belonging to the Bonython estate near the village of Cury, north-east of Mullion itself. At first known simply as Lizard Airship Station, Mullion became Cornwall's centre of airship operations, the surrounding waters witness to a battle fought without quarter for well over two years.

▲ RNAS Mullion, its sheds and windbreaks complete. Four Sopwith 1½ Strutter naval biplanes sit by the small white hangar. Accommodation huts and the canteen are top left (AUTHOR'S COLLECTION).

To house the craft a huge shed was built, over 350 feet long, 100 feet wide and 70 feet high; a slightly smaller version followed in 1917. The shed entrances were given towering windbreaks, to protect the airships from gusts across the exposed heath while moving them in and out. An electricity generator, fitting shop, meteorological hut and wireless cabin appeared, together with a hydrogen-producing gas-plant and gasometer since at that time all airships were hydrogen-filled.

At first, people in the surrounding villages were dubious about the station. Endless noisy lorries bringing materials disturbed livestock and churned up tiny rural lanes. Relations waned further when one of the trucks ran over a pedestrian, though it was later shown the man had been teetering in the road after visiting the local pub. Another broke down a fence and temporarily freed several pigs. Gradually though, the locals grew to respect what they found out about their new neighbours' taxing and dangerous work.

For servicemen, the long rail journey from up-country to their new posting involved a change at Gwinear Road and thence to Helston, from where personnel were picked up by Mullion's Talbot motor-car (for officers) or battered Ford truck (ratings). Most officers were billeted in nearby villages but for the men wooden huts were built on the station. A YMCA cabin also appeared, funded by the Helston and District Allies' Relief Fund Committee and erected by Mr Bennett of Bodmin. At its peak Mullion's complement was around 650 officers and men.

In August 1916 a chance arose for the Navy and locals to mingle, when Mullion personnel took part in a concert supporting the Lizard Lifeboat Fund. Among the station's artistes were Chief Petty Officer Oakes the comedian, and Air Mechanic Longden on the piano. The event was the first of many at which Mullion joined in and eventually a station band was formed. Often its members were excused other duties so they could practise; the ensemble swelled. Mullion's musicians became a popular local attraction, playing at village fêtes and functions across the Lizard.

▲ Mullion men plus mascot prepare for a 'run ashore' on their overloaded Royal Navy lorry. They're off to sample the attractions of Helston (AUTHOR'S COLLECTION).

Aircraft

To work with Cornwall's airships in the U-boat war, the Admiralty created several bases across the Duchy for naval aircraft. Though most aeroplanes couldn't carry the bomb loads of airships they were faster, allowing a quick response to emergencies. A combination was deployed of different aircraft types. Generally landplanes flew inshore patrols; floatplanes and larger flying-boats, the latter built with hulls, were used further out to sea.

Construction of the base known as Royal Naval Air Station Newlyn (Land's End) began late in 1916, using a bulging waterside apron near Newlyn's southern harbour pier. Bessoneau canvas hangars and wooden huts were erected; later a more permanent aircraft shed appeared. To help with the building work, from Gwavas stone quarry across the road a tiny narrow-gauge stream locomotive was borrowed, ironically of German origin. Rails were laid from the station's hard standing down beyond the shoreline, on which a trolley was used to move the water-based wheel-less aircraft across the shingle. Newlyn's first Short Type 184 floatplanes, bearing identifying serials 8049 and 8350, arrived for operations during January 1917.

The station's officers occupied York House at Nancealverne; other ranks were billeted in local cottages. As their daytime lodgings the officers took over a small cottage just behind the station formerly belonging to Tommy Tonkins, a local rope-maker. To allow a view over the base below, two windows were cut into the east-facing bedroom walls. The cottage was passable for a few people but in bad weather became frowsty when a dozen pilots and observers, waiting for clear skies, sat around and smoked. In winter a coal-fire made brave efforts, but gave off sulphurous vapours which mingled with fumes from the kerosene lamps and added to the murk.

On 3 April 1917, Newlyn became part of the newly-formed RNAS South Western Group, which had its headquarters at Mount Wise, Devonport and reported to Commander-in-Chief HM Ships and Vessels Devonport. The Group was created to manage the growing RNAS presence across Cornwall, the south-west of England and south Wales. Its first Commanding Officer was Wing Commander Eugene L Gerrard, a veteran airman who'd learned to fly well before the war. As Newlyn built up its strength, the waterfront apron became so overcrowded that sometimes aircraft were stored in the local Trinity House sheds, their sprawling wings folded back to save space.

▲ RNAS Newlyn/Land's End was built on land near the south pier; three canvas Bessoneaux hangars are in use. Foundations have been laid for a permanent aircraft shed, and just behind the base is the airmen's cottage. Rails mounting a floatplane trolley ran from the station's centre to the waterline (J M BRUCE/G S LESLIE COLLECTION).

▲ Short 184 floatplane N1604 coded 9, seen on RNAS Newlyn's trolley with its crew aboard. It's under power, and between its floats are mounted bombs (J M BRUCE/G S LESLIE COLLECTION).

To provide aerial patrols off north Cornwall's coast the Admiralty sought to build another station, but could find nowhere suitable for water-based aircraft. Consequently a search was made for somewhere to serve as an airfield for landplanes. Just west of Padstow at the hamlet of Crugmeer, near the cliff top, a 50-acre site was requisitioned and a bumpy landing-strip marked out. Exposed to high winds, it wasn't ideal but the best the Admiralty could locate in the area.

Several canvas hangars were put up, with wooden buildings and bell tents as shelter for officers and other ranks respectively. Later some brick-built huts were built, their roofs formed from curved corrugated iron. In March 1918 the new base was commissioned as RNAS Padstow/Crugmeer. Small DH.6 two-seat biplanes began to arrive and Padstow's complement grew to around 180 men. On 31 May 1918, the airfield's No.500 and No.501 Flights began patrols; roughly a dozen aircraft were stationed there. One or two BE2c biplanes also appeared, a two-seater design stemming from pre-war days.

▲ Spring 1918: air and ground crew form up for their photograph at RNAS Padstow/ Crugmeer (AUTHOR'S COLLECTION).

▲ A rare sight at Padstow's airfield, BE2c biplane 9976. It's come to grief in a perimeter hedge, but a couple of days later was flying again; 9976 served at Padstow between May and November 1918 (AUTHOR'S COLLECTION).

In May too a DH.9 flight formed at Padstow. The DH.9 was a better-built, more reliable aeroplane than the old DH.6; in mid-June the new unit was christened No.494 Flight. From August 1918 the Flight fell under No.250 Squadron RAF, at first led by Major R E Orton, but later by Major F Warren Merriam AFC who pre-war had made his name in Falmouth as a motor-car enthusiast.

On the Isles of Scilly, a further station for waterborne aeroplanes was built to carry out anti-submarine patrols over the Atlantic. During January 1917 an RNAS party arrived at Porth Mellon, on the western side of St Mary's. A wooden hangar was put up, concrete hard-standing laid.

However, it was soon found Porth Mellon's billowing waves were sometimes too powerful for safe aero-operations. After a search led by Flight Commander R B Maycock, a less exposed spot was discovered on nearby Tresco at New Grimsby's beach, the land side bounded by Hacket Town Lane, Great Pool and Pool Road, and including buildings belonging to Abbey Farm.

A move from St Mary's was made, and by February 1917 Royal Naval Air Station Tresco was operational. That month the first Curtiss H.12 flying-boats arrived for patrols, large twin-engined biplanes. Serialled 8654, 8652 and 8656, the latter was flown in by the station's new Commanding Officer, Squadron Commander R J J Hope-Vere. Short 184 floatplanes also appeared. On 3 April Tresco too joined the RNAS South Western Group.

At first, like the other stations facilities were scant: canvas hangarage; unloved bell-tent accommodation, a marquee for a mess; a few huts. Local people working in the island's flower trade were experts in screening fields of daffodils, and showed their new neighbours how to protect the tents by creating windbreaks from rushes growing nearby. The more senior service personnel were ferried over daily from billets on St

▲ Early summer 1917: RNAS Tresco under construction. It's early days and the aircraft hangars are yet to be built. The station's concrete slipway has been laid and on the beach are two Curtiss H.12 flying-boats, one being assembled. Behind the aircraft is the wooden fore-body of the *Sophie* (AUTHOR'S COLLECTION).

▲ Royal Naval Air Service Curtiss H.12 flying-boat and admirers seen during 1917, propped up with packing-cases at the top of Tresco's slipway. Huge for its time, the aircraft rests on a simple trolley (AUTHOR'S COLLECTION).

Mary's. In RNAS documentation, even following its move to Tresco the station was sometimes called Port Mellon or worse, Port Melon.

Early that summer the men of the RNAS Air Construction Section arrived, bringing the island's first lorries, and put up a more substantial hangar. Proper accommodation was also built: wooden billets, officers' and sergeants' messes, a sickbay; on the station's south-east side the bell-tents thinned out. A concrete slipway appeared on which rails were laid and a trolley fitted, to launch and retrieve the aircraft. Near the tents an area was cleared in expectation of visits by airships from Mullion.

On the hill above New Grimsby a wireless station took shape, while a small floating dock was used to help with refuelling and maintaining Tresco's aircraft on the water. For a time the base shared its beach with the wrecked prow of *Sophie*, a former Norwegian barque beached back in December 1896 with just a shivering dog aboard; her crew had abandoned ship before she'd been towed in by local vessel *Lady of the Isles*.

Chapter 3 - Home Front

Pulling Together

As Cornwall's men left for distant battlefields, at home another army mustered. The effect of the First World War on civilians was unparalleled, fear and loss reaching out to scar even the tiniest villages. The sheer scale of warfare, the numbers joining up, had never before been seen; everyone knew soldiers, sailors or airmen serving their country. Driven by government too, patriotic energy surged; people on the home front rallied to the war effort, anxious to do what they could to bring the horrible affair to an end.

In scores of Cornish drawing rooms and village halls, meetings were held to arrange collections of useful items for soldiers and sailors: socks, mittens, gloves, bandages. By the end of 1914 a mass of committees and groups had been formed, chiefly by

▲ Cornwall's town and village centres became assembly points for departing soldiers, as those left behind looked on. Here, Padstow's Broad Street late in 1914: soldiers, horses and civilians (Malcolm McCarthy collection).

▶ Gorgeous Wrecks: cap badge from the uniform of the Cornwall Volunteer Training Corps (AUTHOR'S COLLECTION).

women, older men and the church. Distress fund organisers and sewing circles multiplied. First-aid and home nursing classes were set up, while the British Red Cross and St John's Ambulance societies gathered clothing for servicemen. Fruit and vegetables were sent to the DCLI's bulging barracks at Bodmin, to the temporary encampments of soldiers at Falmouth and Truro, and to Scraesdon Fort where they were received gratefully by commanding officer Lieutenant-Colonel Tottie.

The Duchy also became a sanctuary for Belgian refugees, people caught up in the brutal fighting who fled to Britain with nothing; often they were traumatised young widows with children. In January 1915 the Truro Belgian Refugee Committee was created. Over the war years Cornwall's civilians helped with clothes and food, housing and furniture; support never faded.

Public entertainments such as concerts and magic-lantern evenings became frequent, after which the hat would be passed round. Typical was a recital at Helston in October 1916, to support the Trafalgar Day Fund for Orphans of Seamen and Marines. As well as local people, the event was attended by Penzance naval base's commanding officer Lieutenant Commander Blair.

The home front's efforts were reported ceaselessly in Cornwall's newspapers; no bring-and-buy sale or amateur show was too insignificant. Such coverage contrasted sharply with treatment of the military campaigns, reduced to vagueness and optimism by censorship under the Defence of the Realm Act: DORA, as many thought of it. Fund-raising ran right through the war; even as Germany's collapse became inevitable, nine days before the Armistice a recital took place at Stratton's Lecture Hall in aid of the Flying Services Fund. Never was there any sign of good-cause fatigue while during the entertainments, perhaps performers and audiences briefly forgot their awful clutching fear for loved ones overseas.

Over much of the war too Cornwall had its own second-line defence force: the Volunteer Training Corps. The Corps was a national body, a forerunner of the Second World War's Home Guard, and undertook similar duties. Generally its troops were ineligible for front-line service: old soldiers, essential war workers, members of the clergy. As part of their uniform the men wore a red armband bearing the royal initials GR (Georgius Rex), which led to unkind nicknames such as 'Gorgeous Wrecks' and 'God's Rejects'. Nonetheless, many useful tasks were carried out while younger men were freed up for the front.

By mid-1915 Cornish VTC contingents had formed in numerous towns and villages to assist in protecting sensitive areas, particularly along the coast. The men also helped guard national treasures: precious papers including the Domesday Book, which arrived for safe keeping at Bodmin Gaol. That summer as well, the DCLI's recruiting detachment travelled round Cornwall calling for yet more volunteers; the following year would see conscription.

From the outbreak, in Cornwall as elsewhere scare-stories ran wild over German spies. Eavesdropping, counting troops and ships, sending coded messages to the foe; supposed secret agents lurked in every corner.

During August 1914 the court at Falmouth dealt with Johannes Engel, a chandler in the town married to a Penzance woman. Held in custody for a week, suspected spy Hr Engel was acquitted of nefarious activity but as an alien was then re-arrested and detained anyway. In the same month one of the town's many licensees, also German, was charged with possession of guns and ammunition. A further suspicious-looking foreigner, accused of signalling to ships from Budock, was later released; he turned out to be a Danishman who simply enjoyed a pleasant walk.

In December 1915 the author D H Lawrence arrived at Zennor, with his German wife Frieda. At first they lodged at the Tinners' Arms but later rented a nearby cottage named Higher Tregerthen. Local people quickly became distrustful of the couple, believing them spies.

During their clifftop walks Frieda and David took to joyful singing of German songs; added to that, though he loved West Penwith's countryside Lawrence didn't help himself by being openly offensive about Cornish ways. Rumours spread of fuel kept for U-boats below the cliffs by Higher Tregerthen, while it later emerged Frieda was a relative of the German air ace, Baron Manfred von Richthofen. Eventually, local police ordered the pair to leave.

During November 1916, Britain's secret service bureau MI5 made an arrest at Falmouth. Their suspect was a Dutch woman, known for her libidinous lifestyle, which seemed always to favour highly-placed military men: handsome, bold, fashionably elegant Mata Hari.

The former exotic dancer had arrived in Cornwall en route from Spain to Holland, aboard the steamer *Hollandia*. Along with her ten travelling trunks she was taken ashore by George Grant and his wife Janet, both counter-espionage officers stationed in Falmouth. In fact though, and coincidentally, they'd mistaken her for a German agent named Clara Benedix to whom she bore a likeness.

After questioning at the agents' digs in the town, and a visit to Scotland Yard during when her real identity was confirmed, Mata Hari was released for lack of evidence and returned to Spain. But the following year she was arrested in France and allegedly confessed to spying for the Germans; dressed to the nines and refusing a blindfold, she was executed by firing squad.

Cornwall's civilians also collected food and clothing in support of local

◀ In November 1916, mistaken for a German spy, on her arrival at Falmouth Dutch exotic dancer Mata Hari was detained by MI5 (AUTHOR'S COLLECTION).

▲ Like hospitals across Britain, to help deal with the war-wounded Truro's Royal Cornwall Infirmary was pressed into service. On the main steps two nurses take a break (AUTHOR'S COLLECTION).

hospitals. After the terrible battles overseas British casualties were returned home and dispersed nationwide, wherever there were spare hospital beds. In 1916 the Royal Naval Auxiliary Hospital was created in Truro's workhouse at the top of Tregolls Road, initially with 150 beds; the usual inmates were moved out. Already, since June 1915 the Royal Cornwall Infirmary at Truro had been treating wounded servicemen.

More hospital facilities were pressed into use at Falmouth, Launceston and Penzance, as well as Camborne, Fowey, Newquay and Scorrier. Local people opened canteens for the walking wounded, and many welcomed recuperating men into their homes. Schools and public halls were requisitioned for additional temporary nursing care; some reached a dreadful longevity.

As the fighting dragged on, those at home began to experience shortages of goods and food while prices rose. 1916's harvest was poor, the potato crop failed, shipping losses increased. Even in Cornwall supplies of bread, meat and fish began to dwindle; sugar became a luxury. A shortage of saffron forced bakers to use other means of colouring their Cornish saffron buns.

Quests for frugality were launched. Eggs were carefully collected, their quotas logged and allowances drawn up. Trigging, harvesting cockles along the shore, grew in popularity; small prawns were also gathered. By 1916 Stithians' famous agricultural show had been abandoned. In April 1918 ration cards appeared for butter and meat while across the Duchy shops began to open only for limited hours, and sometimes closed altogether.

At Gorran that summer Mingo the butcher, who slaughtered his own animals, feared he'd be unable to supply any more meat to the area. His sons had gone to the war – one had died – and he simply had no available labour to prepare the beasts. Tobacco became scarce at times, which more and more affected Cornish women as well as men. Pub opening hours were cut, ale was watered down, old soaks cried in their beer.

Meanwhile, travel and movement controls had been brought in. Along coastal railway stretches, between dusk and dawn carriages had their blinds drawn to ensure no lights shone to seaward. Parts of Cornwall's coastline, particularly near military bases, were made off-limits to civilians. Restrictions were severe; Newlyn-based artist Laura Knight was criticised by coastguards when she painted a view of St Ives harbour. Though small red permit books allowing sketching later became available, fearful of being called a spy she retreated to her Lamorna studio. Hiding in bushes, Laura stealthily drew spring pictures of gorse and early flowers.

But the law didn't stop Marjorie Williams of Gorran, married to a London-based barrister. The couple wrote devotedly, and in August 1917 she noted in her letter: "A wonderful convoy went along the eastern horizon … I think there were 24: all merchantmen steamers and two bigger ones … with a circle

◀ This lady is dressed in the uniform of a VAD nurse, and came from the St Agnes area. The photo was taken just post-war; she's wearing her British War Medal (to our left), and Victory Medal (AUTHOR'S COLLECTION).

of eight or nine destroyers … and the airship up above, in front." Unthinking rather than a deliberate breach of DORA of course, but what would the local watchers and amateur spy-catchers have made of Marjorie's description?

Industry

▲ In a cramped ward, nurses attend wounded servicemen at Liskeard Cottage Hospital (AUTHOR'S COLLECTION).

By 1914, from its mid-Victorian heyday Cornish mining output had plummeted, but urgent wartime demand for tin revived fortunes somewhat; wolfram and arsenic were also extracted. A temporary mini-boom took place as the miners recovered as much ore as possible in the shortest time. But many mineworkers joined up; in France they found themselves much in demand. Often they became military engineers, or sappers, their underground skills adapted to trench warfare and tunnelling beneath enemy lines to plant explosives.

Not surprisingly, Cornish fishing suffered severely. Many fishermen left at the outbreak, while the Duchy's waters quickly became perilous. Trawlers not taken by the Admiralty were the most dilapidated while despite plans, often the remaining vessels weren't escorted by naval craft while working. Over the summer of 1917 though, numerous fishing boats were given 3- or 6-pounder guns and joined the newly-created Fishery Reserve, a sub-section of the RNR's Trawler Section. From then, if possible the boats fished in groups of which some were armed to protect the others.

Cornwall's holiday industry too was hard-hit; Bude, Falmouth and Newquay all experienced big drops in hotel and boarding-house bookings. Family breaks were shelved while the man of the house was away, coastal resorts suffered as wild fears grew of invasion or bombardment from the sea. January 1917 saw the *Newquay Express* advertising insurance of local properties from zeppelin bombing raids, available from newsagents Trethewy & Sons of Mount Charles, St Austell. By the summer though, perhaps after salvos from local hoteliers, the *Express* conceded such raids were unlikely.

Inland at the Duchy's industrial heart, Holman Brothers Ltd of Camborne was a renowned engineering company and by 1914 supplied mining machinery across the world. The war began tragically for the Holman family, who lost director John's young soldier son Jack, killed in France with the 4th Royal Irish Dragoon Guards. John's brother Treve joined the Royal Flying Corps and served in Mesopotamia. Though demand for mining equipment didn't fall off as might have been expected, Holmans soon began to concentrate on war work while its labour force changed radically.

▲ Cligga Head, Perranporth: Nobel Group factory workers, 1916. Several women are wearing the company's triangular war service badges, and some are in mourning (AUTHOR'S COLLECTION).

Cornwall's fuse manufacturers, which had grown around the mining industry, became inundated with work. Bickford, Smith & Co's factory at Tuckingmill near Camborne, and the nearby Roskear site of William Bennetts, Sons & Co churned out ingredients for artillery shell fuses, while new works were opened at Redruth close to the brewery. On Camborne's cricket ground, magazines were built to house the fuse explosives. Fuse jobs were dangerous; workers toiled separately and in silence.

Meanwhile, on the cliff top at Cligga Head outside Perranporth, mothballed factories once owned by the British and Colonial Explosives Company were resuscitated. Under the Nobel Group, the site produced grenade ingredients and again, fuses; nearly 1,000 people worked there. Near Two Waters Foot outside Liskeard, Burrowite Explosives Ltd at Trago Mills made blasting explosive, used in charging land-mines.

Dangerous war work also took place amid the towans at Hayle, where the National Explosives Company had been founded in 1888 to produce dynamite for mining. With demand down for commercial explosives the factory had turned to War Office and Admiralty contracts, becoming a leading supplier to the services.

▲ A small wooden cartridging hut at Hayle's National Explosives Company; peeping out are two women workers. The huts were surrounded by banks of earth to minimise damage across the site if an accident occurred (AUTHOR'S COLLECTION).

▲ Industrial landscape at Hayle Towans' National Explosives Company. The buildings are set far apart from one another in case of a blast (AUTHOR'S COLLECTION).

▲ Holman's of Camborne: with baggy overalls, and caps keeping their hair back, female workers line up for a group photograph with male colleagues (AUTHOR'S COLLECTION).

Hayle produced huge quantities of ammunition cordite, as well as guncotton charges for torpedoes and mines. While soldiers of the 3rd (Reserve) Battalion DCLI guarded the factory's perimeter, National grew to employ around 1,800 people. All told, at its wartime peak over 3,000 people worked for Cornwall's explosives makers.

Despite the greatly increased work in such a hazardous place, during the war just two serious explosions occurred at National and only four people were killed. In the same accident during December 1916, two men and two women died. Cissie Rogers and May Stoneman, aged 20 and 21, were laid to rest in Phillack churchyard, their war service acknowledged; Cissie was buried on Christmas Eve.

Women At War

With so many men fighting overseas, at home Cornwall's women came forward. At first, they devoted long hours to providing knitted garments for soldiers and sailors, or helped organise events raising funds for servicemens' comforts. Women collected unwanted clothes to sell or pass on to the troops, and grimly sewed hessian sandbags for use at the front.

Before the war, one of the few careers not dominated by men was nursing. As Cornwall's wartime hospitals grew so too did the numbers of women who cared for wounded servicemen. Nursing organisations swelled, among them the

◀ From mid-1918, at RNAS Newlyn personnel from the Women's Royal Naval Service worked alongside male ground crew. For tasks like aircraft doping or servicing, requiring her uniform be protected, this lady wears loose cotton overalls. Behind, a Short 184 floatplane (AUTHOR'S COLLECTION).

▲ Holman's female workers toil in the engineering shop. What would today's health and safety edicts make of their exposed machines and the flapping drive-belts? (AUTHOR'S COLLECTION).

Queen Alexandra's Imperial Military Nursing Service, the Territorial Force Nursing Service and the nationwide Voluntary Aid Detachments.

With the shortage of men, at Truro's Royal Naval Auxiliary Hospital the VAD women took up stretcher-bearing for cot cases; their labours were publicly recognised in the British Journal of Nursing. At Christmas times, nurses who weren't on duty turned in anyway to help keep patients' spirits up, chatting or playing cards with them. Many women received commendations for their nursing work, among them 27-year-old Winifred Whitworth of Truro, acknowledged late in 1918 by the *London Gazette* for 'valuable service in connection with the war'.

Increasingly too, women filled places left by men in industry and agriculture. As part of a national initiative which saw the Land Army emerge, in 1915 the Cornwall War Agricultural Committee was formed to boost local food production and persuade more women to work in farming. The Committee covered nine district educational areas;

▲ J&F Pool munitions workers, nearly all women, assembled at the Hayle factory for their group photograph (GORDIE HOLLOW COLLECTION).

female speakers arrived from up-country to promote the cause, demonstrations were given by women of ploughing and other agricultural labour.

That year 25 women classified as 'moveable', that's to say prepared to work anywhere in Cornwall, came forward to the Committee's Truro and Falmouth branches, with 15 other full-time and more than 70 part-time volunteers. For long hours they toiled at the harvest, as well as longer-term farm jobs: milking cows, collecting eggs, cleaning out pigs.

On the big estates as well, at times women replaced men. By 1918, softwood from Lanhydrock was being used increasingly in Cornish mines. This led to employment of Cornish women on the estate, who worked at cross-cutting and faggoting.

Some of the Duchy's surviving mines also recruited females, latter-day bal maidens, for surface work; among them was Menheniot's Wheal Mary Anne. Dolcoath and Levant too kept women on for the duration, mostly labouring at the stamps, or roasting tin ore in calciners to extract the arsenic. During 1917 Polpuff Glass Mine at St Dennis reopened and women hammered at the cut blocks of granite to help isolate the feldspar content, used in manufacture of electrical porcelain. In the clay industry too females found jobs, gruelling shifts washing out clay from pit bottoms at the Rocks site at Bugle, and Gothers China Clay Works near St Dennis. At Little Treviscoe, close to St Stephens, they helped bag up ground china clay.

In the towns, Cornish engineering companies employed women. Often factories offered better conditions, more interesting work and greater freedom than, say, domestic service. Consistently though women were paid maybe half the men's wages, while their hours were equally long and the jobs sometimes hazardous.

Holmans of Camborne churned out hundreds of howitzer base plates, together with depth-charge throwers for the Navy, machine-gun parts and later, tank engines. As male employees left, women stepped into shop-floor jobs using machine-tools; some became inspectors, others worked in the offices. In all Holman employed around 200 females, some of the factory floor staff toiling in three shifts.

Camborne's fuse factories

◀ Miss Clemence, a young wartime machine-operator with J&F Pool (JOHN BENNETT).

took scores of women, as did the explosives manufacturers at Hayle Towans, Perranporth and Two Waters Foot. The J&F Pool metalworking concern of Hayle also turned to producing munitions, many of their workers female. At National's Hayle site and Nobel's at Perranporth, the women worked in remote cabins making tubes of dynamite and gelignite. As well as the strain inherent in their tasks, they endured frequent sickness and cumulative skin discolouration caused by chemicals used in the explosives.

At the explosives factories, those with jobs in hazardous areas had to wear slippers or rubber boots. Each morning before starting, females were searched by a matron for any object that might cause a fatal spark. Eventually two National women were trained at the Camborne School of Mines and employed in the company's quality control laboratories; truly a case of breaking down doors protecting male preserves.

▲ Padstow women set up a tea market for service personnel visiting the port. Several seamen are from visiting battleship HMS *Conqueror*, which moored at the mouth of the Camel (MALCOLM MCCARTHY COLLECTION).

Chapter 4 - Operations

Around The Coastline

SHORTLY AFTER WAR **came, at Falmouth shipping restrictions had been introduced. Movements in and out of harbour were forbidden without special licences issued by the Custom House; initially fishing and rowing-boats were exempt, but from 1915 the fishing fleet had to comply. Mercantile movements were generally made in daylight and a blackout was introduced. The Admiralty requisitioned tugs and various other vessels, and after an Act of Parliament was passed also took over management of the town's docks.**

Early in 1915 Falmouth's naval presence was briefly increased when a shoal of converted minesweepers assembled, before sailing for the Mediterranean and the Dardanelles; some had originated from Cornwall's fisher fleets. The following year, four days before Christmas sadly local ex-trawler *St Ives* was sunk. Given a small gun and renumbered Admiralty No.1192, *St Ives* had become an Auxiliary Patrol Vessel helping guard the remaining fishermen, but struck a mine 3 miles off St Anthony Point near Falmouth. Twelve crewmen died and the explosion was heard several miles away.

▲ His Majesty's Hospital Ship *Glenart Castle* off Cornwall's coastline. Requisitioned in September 1914, during February 1918 she was torpedoed by submarine UC-56 near Lundy Island and sank with great loss of life (MALCOLM McCARTHY COLLECTION).

▲ Wearing a drab camouflage scheme to help disguise her profile, this British merchantman is aground off Tolcarne beach, Newquay (MALCOLM MCCARTHY COLLECTION).

▲ Built by Harvey's of Hayle, RMS *Lyonesse* served with the West Cornwall Steamship Co Ltd. For most of the war she braved the U-boats, taking passengers and cargo between Penzance and St Mary's (AUTHOR'S COLLECTION).

In a notorious action during the late afternoon of 22 February 1917, submarine U-21 (*Kapitänleutnant* Hersing) sank six neutral Dutch ships off the Isles of Scilly, west of Bishop Rock. The vessels had put in at Falmouth, and before continuing on to Philadelphia had been assured of safe passage by the German authorities. Taking to their boats, the surviving crewmen were spotted from the shore; at once the lifeboat service and Navy were notified. St Agnes lifeboat *Charles Deere James* found two boats, which each took aboard a lifeboatman as pilot for the brief journey to St Mary's. The search broadened; Scilly-based craft located other boats and around 300 men were saved.

In April 1917 the RNR minesweeping trawler *Star of Freedom* hit a mine off Trevose Head and was lost with 10 crewmen. The same month, SS *Ballarat*, a former P&O liner pressed as an Australian troopship and transport, was torpedoed by submarine UB-32 off Wolf Rock. In an effort to save her she was taken in tow by a destroyer and the drifter *Midge*, but the following day sank off the Lizard. Everyone aboard was rescued, nearly 1,800 people; even pets were brought off but the cargo went down, including gold bullion.

By that time Falmouth was busier than ever, home to a sizeable minesweeper force while the convoy system of defending merchant shipping was just coming into use; clusters of vessels would gather outside the harbour to embark under protection of the Navy. During May 1917, Rear-Admiral John Luard was appointed Rear-Admiral Falmouth, the port's Senior Naval Officer.

▲ In November 1918, camouflaged American coaster *Lake Harris* came to grief at Longrock east of Penzance, but was successfully refloated. On her poop is mounted a small defensive gun (MALCOLM McCARTHY COLLECTION).

▲ Crewmen from visiting battleship *Conqueror* arrive for a spell of shore leave at Padstow. Local people have turned out to greet them (MALCOLM McCARTHY COLLECTION).

The town's ship repair work too became enormously important. In 1916 the Admiralty had decided to build a new dry-dock known as No.3, bigger than the existing pair, though it was two years before plans were finally agreed and construction began. Wharfage too was extended. Ships awaiting repair or adaptation, mercantile and naval, moored upriver in the deep meandering Carrick Roads.

But the dock's labour force and facilities were too small to cope with the spiralling workload. In 1918 the Admiralty requested a London firm of ship repairers, R H Green and Silley Weir, to look into the backlog. Additional workers were sent to help clear the congestion; meanwhile Green and Silley Weir grasped Falmouth's potential and later that year bought the yard. More skilled men arrived from the Royal Albert Docks, while new workshops and machinery appeared.

Throughout the war the St Mawes Steam Tug and Passenger Company Ltd kept its service between St Mawes Quay and Falmouth, using passenger tug *Roseland*. Meanwhile, among the more unusual arrivals were steamships *Iris* and *Daffodil*, former Mersey ferryboats. The pair had been damaged in the Navy's raid of April 1918 on the German-held Belgian port of Zeebrugge; they'd acted as troop landing ships. During the repair work at Falmouth both were opened to visitors, and many people came to view their battle-scars.

Wearde Quay

On the River Lynher, HMS *Defiance* continued its exercises with deadly torpedoes and sea-mines. Live firings of both took place mostly in Whitsand and Cawsand Bays, at times held up as maritime traffic passed in and out of Plymouth. Civilians were discouraged from watching the great explosions; parts of eastern Cornwall's coast had become areas of restricted access.

Wearde Quay received occasional British submarines, from the old A Class to the somewhat less dangerous D Class, the surface-power engines of which ran on diesel rather than petrol. Over 1917 and 1918 His Majesty's Australian Ship *Platypus* also appeared on the Lynher, a submarine depot vessel used to store equipment, weapons and provisions for the undersea craft, which were too small to carry much themselves. By then though she was redundant in her original role; both Australia's submarines had been lost.

▲ Hauling practice with sea mines at HMS *Defiance*; these are dummies, but the base conducted many live exercises off the Cornish coast (STEVE JOHNSON/CYBERHERITAGE).

▲ HMAS *Platypus* at rest on the River Lynher; British D Class submarine D3 is moored alongside. On 12 March 1918 D3 was sunk with all 29 hands by a French airship which mistook her for a U-boat (AUTHOR'S COLLECTION).

Naval Motor Launches

Soon after war began, it became all too clear Britain's coastal defenders suffered from a severe shortage of naval patrol vessels. The Admiralty began an urgent search for more craft, small and fast, to hunt the U-boats. Their quest ended in the United States, at the Electric Launch Company's shipyard in Bayonne, New Jersey.

To meet the Admiralty's requirement ELCO turned out kits for hundreds of motor launches, assembled in Canada to avoid embarrassing American neutrality and dispatched as deck cargo aboard merchant ships. Known simply as MLs, the new boats were wooden with twin petrol engines, armed with depth charges and a quick-firing 1- or 3-pounder deck gun; they could manage almost 20 knots. Two versions were produced, one of 75 feet and 34 tons, most of 80 feet and 37 tons. Altogether, the Navy ordered 550.

But capable mariners were at a premium. For its ML crews the Admiralty was forced to look widely; increasingly, those with no previous sea experience were accepted. Training saw many accidents; regular naval instructors wept as brand-new boats were driven into piers or each other by young men more accustomed to handling motor-bikes. It was said some ML skippers stuck out their right arm when turning to starboard, the left for port. But following hurried preparation, straight away the raw crews were sent to hunt the enemy. Against them, onslaught from wind and sea, navigation along dark or foggy coasts, and the submarines themselves, fitted with deck guns and capable of fighting it out on the surface.

MLs were deployed along much of Britain's coast, and the first of the Penzance contingent arrived over the summer of 1916; His Majesty's Motor Launch ML319. Penzance's MLs came under control of Admiralty Patrol Area XIV, a zone jutting south and west from Cornwall. A wireless link with Falmouth's command centre ensured orders were received promptly but the westernmost crews operated with spirited independence, often putting to sea on the off-chance of spotting the enemy. Some crews made modifications to their boats, not least to reduce the racket from the engine exhausts which notified their presence to any surfaced U-boat for miles around. Others lashed canvas dodgers over their cockpits, to keep off the worst of the incessant, drenching sea spray.

▲ On the deck of their small craft, the crewmen of Newlyn-based ML245 pose for the camera. MLs had a crew of ten: two officers and eight seamen (MALCOLM MCCARTHY COLLECTION).

▲ ML351 at the entrance to N Holman's dock, Penzance. Inside the dock gates divers are in the water, while civilians watch proceedings from beyond (AUTHOR'S COLLECTION).

By 1916 Mount's Bay had become congested with merchantmen and naval craft. Like Falmouth, Penzance was a key supply link with France and during the war thousands of vessels passed through; the MLs had to squeeze in as best they could. Before long most of them had moved to the bay's western side, mucking in with Newlyn's remaining fishing-boats and tying up at the North Pier.

To keep them supplied, the Navy co-opted the *Dreel Castle*, an armed drifter of 97 tons originally registered at Kirkcaldy and commissioned during February 1915. Converted into a depot ship and based at Falmouth, *Dreel Castle* plodded a monotonous route to Penzance and the small naval outpost at St Mary's, ensuring motor launches and auxiliaries were replenished with fuel, arms, equipment and rations.

The MLs were found fairly durable but they sailed so frequently, often in poor weather, that at times they had to come out of the water for substantial repairs. Maintenance was generally carried out locally, either alongside, beached at Newlyn or for bigger jobs, berthed in Holman's dry dock. And as the launches spread their patrols wider, at Padstow on the north coast another outstation was formed.

Some of the work became routine; regular but vital tasks. Over the long years, escorts to hundreds of merchantmen; laying off net defences in attempts to snare the submarines; placing sea-mines in shallow waters where large vessels couldn't operate. Life at sea was harsh and often the sailors lived on cold food; in rough conditions their craft rolled and bucketed, which made it impossible to hold even a pot of tea on the galley stove.

Duffel-coated but soaked and chilled, to conserve fuel the crews would stop engines, drifting for hours while all aboard scanned the water for signs of a submarine: an oil trail, a passing shadow beneath the waves, the feathered wake from a periscope breaking the surface. From time to time stray mines were spied, attempts made to detonate them with rifle-fire in light-hearted competitions among the sailors. Occasionally too they would spot wreckage from a torpedoed vessel, or rescue exhausted men found drifting in lifeboats. But the main job, always, was stalking the submarines.

During the late afternoon of 12 December 1917, in murky conditions south-west of the Lizard, Newlyn-based ML357 stumbled on a surfaced U-boat. In command,

▲ ML350 leaves Newlyn harbour for a patrol. On her foredeck is mounted a 3-pounder gun, aft are depth-charges (AUTHOR'S COLLECTION).

▲ Royal Navy MLs alongside Newlyn's North Pier; all but the far right carry depth charges. Lt Kitson's ML357, second left, was badly damaged after deliberately ramming a U-boat (MALCOLM McCARTHY COLLECTION).

Lieutenant F J B Kitson tried to bring his deck gun to bear. There was no time to move into position. Kitson didn't hesitate. Flat out, he aimed his wooden craft at the enemy's steel conning-tower. He struck a glancing blow; the ML slewed along the submarine's forward deck and plunged back into the dark sea, by good fortune emerging at an attitude from which its gun could be trained.

Kitson's crew let fly; driven off, the U-boat submerged. But ML357 was damaged, making water fast and settling by the stern. Luckily, wireless contact was made with nearby armed tug *Hercules IV*; the launch was taken in tow and hurriedly beached at Penzance. ML357 was repaired and rejoined the patrols, while for his gallantry Kitson received the Distinguished Service Cross.

Just before midnight on 9 April 1918, a French steamer bound for England was torpedoed off the Lizard and sank in three minutes. MLs joined the search for survivors; seven sailors were saved. Two months later, to boost the anti-U-boat campaign new craft arrived at Mount's Bay, with overseas crews. These were Submarine Chaser motor launches of the United States Navy. Like the British MLs they tied up at Newlyn's North Quay: vessels SC.41, 91, 137, 258 and 345 are known to have served. The

▲ ML319 anchored off Tresco, 1917, some of her crew on deck. Later in life she acquired a simple cover over her helm (AUTHOR'S COLLECTION).

American launches were slightly larger than the British MLs, with more depth-charges at the stern and a bigger cockpit.

On the afternoon of 7 September an aircraft from RNAS Tresco spotted the former White Star liner *Persic*, by then a troop-ship carrying American soldiers, which had been crippled by a submarine west of Scilly. Among the vessels arriving to help were MLs 351 and 352, and SC.137; the *Persic* was safely taken in tow. On 11 October, MLs joined an attack by aircraft and armed trawlers on a U-boat south of the islands. Their crews released several depth charges stuffed with TNT and subsequently oil was seen on the surface, a sign the submarine had been damaged. This was one of the final actions in the area.

▲ During the summer of 1918, United States Navy Submarine Chaser motor launches arrived at Newlyn. Here's SC345 off the southern Cornish coast (MALCOLM MCCARTHY COLLECTION).

▲ Mud-berthed at Padstow's naval outstation are a gaggle of MLs, probably during 1918. From the left: ML350, 334, 245, 357, 321 and 570 (MALCOLM MCCARTHY COLLECTION).

But really, it was the deterrent value of the MLs which helped most in the U-boat battle. Their greatest success was in helping to keep the submarines submerged, fearful of terrible concussion or even destruction from depth-charges, and so unable to find their merchantmen targets. The possibility of attack from above was acknowledged by the Germans as a menace which blunted their effectiveness, and added greatly to the tension inherent in U-boat operations.

Airships: Mullion and Bude

Mullion's first airship was one of the new Coastal Class; it was numbered C.9 and began operations on 1 July 1916. The Coastals employed a boxy open-top gondola for the crew, slung beneath a huge trilobe gas-bag (or envelope) just under 200 feet long. Two engines were set one at each end of the gondola, usually 150 hp water-cooled Sunbeams. Top speed was around 50 mph in theory, though the great craft were susceptible to wind currents.

Typically five crewmen were carried: pilot, coxswain, observer, wireless/telegraphy operator and mechanic/engineer. By the aerial standards of the day, the Coastal's

▶ July 1916: airship C.9 after being hit by 'friendly' fire from British troops while patrolling over Jersey. Slowly deflating, she made it back as far as Mullion harbour; the following month, repaired, she returned to service (AUTHOR'S COLLECTION).

armament was fearsome: three or more machine-guns and either bombs or depth-charges. Sluggish on the helm but generally dependable even in bad weather, The C Class saw more action than any other type of British airship, and Mullion's were among the busiest in the RNAS.

Spotting submarines from high up was difficult, but occasionally in clear conditions the dark shadow of a hull might be made out just below the surface. Generally the airships flew at around 2,000 feet, which was felt ideal for surveying the water as efficiently as possible. Sometimes oil leaks were noticeable while of course, a torpedo wake was a sure indicator.

But the real worth of the airships' patrols, like the efforts of their naval colleagues on the surface, was the caginess they caused among U-boat commanders in pressing home attacks. The key to the whole anti-submarine campaign, easier to recognise with hindsight than at the time, was maintaining an uninterrupted flow of merchant shipping; sinking U-boats wasn't an absolute necessity provided they weren't allowed to strike at the vital supply lanes.

Several Coastals flew from Mullion. Their patrol area eventually extended from Plymouth to west and south of Scilly, as well as covering the waters off north Cornwall. Flying took place whenever the weather allowed, seven days a week; often patrols were made along with destroyers, MLs and armed trawlers. Mullion's wireless and direction-

▲ C.9's gondola, looking aft. Her commander, Flight Lieutenant J G Struthers, holds his binoculars ready to search the sea; to our left is a large plate camera. Aft, the wireless operator and mechanic are about their business while above bulges the airship's giant gas-bag (IAN STRATFORD).

finding equipment helped draw the airships to potential targets, though the new-fangled gear had the infuriating habit of breaking at vital times.

For those aboard, the missions were shattering. Flights could last from dawn to dusk. Conditions were bitterly cold, while crews were exposed to the ceaseless din of clattering engines; their only means of communicating were inefficient speaking-tubes or sign-language. Some men made small ovens run off the engine exhaust, in which they'd heat the day's food; otherwise it was bacon sandwiches, boiled eggs and flasks of stewed tea. Back at base with stiff and frozen limbs, at times the flyers had to be helped down from their gondolas by kindly ground crew.

With off-duty activities narrowed by isolation, Mullion's men were thrown onto their own resources. Fads came and went: efforts at rabbit-snaring; allotments; archery against noisy crows, though with no recorded success. Within the main airship shed a tennis court was marked out, while the accommodation huts played each other and the outside world at football and cricket. June 1917 was marked by a particularly crushing win against a Camborne XI, all out for 11 runs and doubtless well under-strength.

Fishing was another popular pastime while the Bonython estate and surrounding farms provided apples, butter, milk and cream. Many of Mullion's personnel bought the Lizard's serpentine ware, including vases, paperweights and egg-cups made by Mr Samuel Jose of Lizard Village. And during their stay too, several naval men met and married local maids.

'Runs ashore' seem to have favoured Penzance, rather than Helston where shops were too often shut and the tennis courts deemed poor. Penzance's Central Hotel and on the front, the Mount's Bay Hotel were favourite places where Mullion's officers met up for social high jinks with their counterparts from Newlyn.

Cornish airship Coastal Class 9 took part in many actions, destroying one U-boat for certain and probably damaging at least three others. She held one of the best operational records of any RNAS airship, and for much of her time was captained by Flight Lieutenant J G Struthers.

Early in February 1917, watching the waters off the Lizard, Struthers spotted the possible wake of a U-boat. By Aldis lamp and Morse code he notified nearby armed trawlers of the enemy below, then began his attack. Struthers dropped his biggest bomb, a 230-pounder, at the head of the submarine's assumed path; despite a thorough search though, no signs were seen of damage.

▲ C.9's crew photographed in front of Mullion's great airship shed doors during 1917; Flight Lieutenant Struthers is sitting to our left (AUTHOR'S COLLECTION).

A few days later, on 12 February, Struthers made a strike off Cape Cornwall after spying a U-boat trailing oil and bubbles. At once he attacked with bombs, while three armed trawlers arrived and released their depth-charges. Later the trawlers found wreckage, which it was thought may have come from the enemy.

In March though, C.9's crew suffered a thoroughly alarming experience. Escorting merchant ships near Plymouth, the airship's aft engine caught fire; flames licked up toward its hydrogen-filled envelope. To avoid the imminent catastrophe of a terrible explosion, crewman Air Mechanic Parkes at once bestraddled the engine, smothering the fire with his body while dousing it with an extinguisher. C.9 limped home on its remaining engine, but valiant Parkes seems to have received no official recognition of his bravery and, his trousers ruined, had to buy another pair with his own money.

During May, Mullion's Meteorological Officer, Sub-Lieutenant Norman Silvester RNVR, moved from the station to a comfortable hut at Drytree, near Goonhilly. He felt the spot would be better suited for his instruments and readings, while he could also run his own small realm in unsupervised peace. To make his daily trip, several times Silvester requested a motorcycle but Mullion's usually amiable commanding officer, Squadron Commander Reginald Colmore, eventually granted him just a bicycle.

On 22 June a destroyer from Plymouth spotted a U-boat 15 miles south of Start Point. Struthers and C.9, flying nearby, arrived to drop a 65 lb delayed-action bomb; the destroyer added two depth-charges. Following that action, Mullion's wireless station monitored German broadcasts and it was noted that calls to the U-boat from its base went unanswered.

By that summer the airships' work had become more harmonised with those on the surface. The new convoy system improved protection for merchant vessels, and Falmouth became an assembly port for outbound groups. On 13 August 1917, Flight Lieutenant Struthers was mentioned in despatches for his attacks and escort work, and for having flown well over 1,000 hours on patrol.

During mid-August C.9 was patrolling near the Eddystone lighthouse when Struthers spied an upturned hull; torpedoed cargo ship SS *Claverley*. A lifeboat was spotted, occupied by five men of whom three were still alive; another man was seen in the water. Struthers transmitted: 'Large capsized steamer. Men alive in waterlogged lifeboat.

▲ Autumn 1917: off the Lizard peninsula Coastal airship C.23a keeps a watchful eye over the seas. Below, a ragged convoy labours eastward (AUTHOR'S COLLECTION).

Remaining over till marked. Assistance at once'. He signalled those below to tell them help was on the way, and attracted the attention of nearby trawlers. The fortunate survivors were landed at Plymouth.

On 21 September Struthers left Mullion at 5.00 am, and settled in for a long beat off the Lizard. South of the point the French steamer *Rouang* appeared, escorted by an armed trawler, having just been torpedoed. Again a hunt began: five hours later a U-boat was detected, surfaced south-east of the Lizard and heading toward a Falmouth-bound convoy. At once, C.9 gave chase.

The submarine saw him and began its crash-dive. Struthers dropped two delayed-action 100 lb bombs ahead of the periscope's final swirl; a violent explosion brought great bubbles of air and oil to the surface. Struthers waited for more signs of the U-boat's demise but finally had to return to Mullion for fuel; while he was there, he loaded more bombs. Meanwhile replacement airships C.2 and C.23a reconnoitred above the scene of the action. Castle class trawler No.3537 HMS *Laverock* and the auxiliary minesweeper *Fusilier* joined the search.

When C.9 returned at 5.00 pm Struthers found an oil slick covering almost a square mile of sea, its position 16 miles south-south-east of the Lizard. *Laverock* swept the water for wreckage until 6.30 pm without result, but noted the presence on the surface of a refined form of oil such as petrol or paraffin. The following day a trawler at the spot momentarily recovered a piece of steel plate in its nets; it became clear to the hunters that C.9 had destroyed the submarine, one of very few airships ever to have sunk a U-boat without help from surface craft. On 2 October Struthers was awarded the Distinguished Service Cross.

1917 saw C.9 complete 1,042 hours 42 minutes of operational flying. Finally, on 14 September 1918 she was deflated for an inspection but the following month was deemed beyond further repair. C.9 had flown a total of 3,720 hours and an estimated 68,200 miles, more than any other airship in the Royal Naval Air Service. By contrast, sister-ship C.10 lasted less than four months, delivered to Mullion on 19 June 1916 and written off after an accident there on 10 October.

Other Mullion Coastals had their moments. During a patrol on 9 September 1916, C.10 was off the Lizard when two burning ships were spotted. A U-boat was also seen, diving while the airship was still some distance away. Bombs were released but the submarine survived and later resurfaced; attacked by the destroyer *Foyle* it disappeared again, and no further sighting was made.

▲ Coastal airship C.2. Its ground crew are using ropes to manhandle the great craft across the ground. In the background, cows graze (AUTHOR'S COLLECTION).

On 12 February 1917, C.22 spied a Norwegian ship with lowered boats 10 miles ESE of Falmouth, along with the wreck of a second vessel. By flash-lamp the airship's commander, Flight Sub-Lieutenant C S Coltson, learned the steamer had been torpedoed. Hoping the culprit had stayed nearby, he began a search along with trawlers 436 *John C Meikle* and 1995 *Gavina*. The careless U-boat was found surfaced only a short distance way, travelling west. As Coltson moved at full speed to attack he was seen, and the enemy started to dive.

From 1,000 ft Coltson dropped a bomb just ahead of the U-boat's path; infuriatingly it was a dud. Helm hard over, at once C.22 released a second bomb which worked correctly; a mass of oil surfaced. The airship stayed on watch but of the submarine there was no sign; Coltson felt his second bomb had probably done its grim job. Unfortunately both his engines began to misbehave so he returned to Mullion, landing just after 3.00 pm in poor visibility and drizzle.

A further action took place on 9 August 1917 as airship C.2 was escorting a convoy over the Atlantic approach to the Channel. A surfaced U-boat was spotted trailing the ships; absorbed in its task, it stayed up until C.2 was only two miles away but then crash-dived. The airship dropped two 100 lb bombs, 200 and 300 yards ahead of the submarine's predicted course; four destroyers joined the search and oil was spotted on the surface. No further sign was seen of the U-boat and the convoy passed safely.

On the murky afternoon of 17 November 1917, Flight Lieutenant R L Montagu's C.23a was east of Dodman Point near Mevagissey when a suspected submarine trail was sighted. Montagu overflew the trail's head and dropped two 100 lb bombs, the

▲ Some of Mullion's ship's company clamber up an airship shed door for a novel group photograph, 1918 (AUTHOR'S COLLECTION).

explosions of which were followed by air bubbles on the surface. Converted trawler *Flintshire*, meanwhile, having seen the attack, made for the spot at full speed. She released three depth charges; passing ML331 added two more. The airship remained watching over the sea until darkness, returning to Mullion after nearly 10 hours, but it was never confirmed a submarine had been sunk.

C.23a served until the spring of 1918, when she was lost in strange circumstances. On 10 May she was patrolling off Newquay at around 400 feet. As she passed over Crantock Bay suddenly a U-boat surfaced, its crew quickly deploying their powerful deck gun. Before scores of shoreline onlookers, the German sailors opened up at their aerial foe. C.23a folded in two and fell into the bay.

The airship's commander, its coxswain, engineer and observer were rescued by local fishing boats; sadly, the wireless operator was lost. Before reinforcements could arrive the U-boat made off, while C.23a was recovered and towed into Newquay harbour. When the wreckage was examined it was found that as well as having been shot at, the airship's gas-bag had developed a fault in flight, causing it to deflate. She never flew again.

A later airship type also flew from Mullion: the Submarine Scout Zero (SSZ) Class. Ten examples served there at different times, the first arriving in July 1917. Smaller than the Coastal, the SSZ had just one engine, a 75 hp Rolls-Royce Hawk, and carried either two 110 lb bombs or a single 250-pounder. Three crewmen sat in the small gondola: a wireless/telegraphy operator, who also manned the nose machine-gun; the pilot in the central position; and aft, by his engine, the air mechanic. Many long patrols were flown but few actions have come down to us; recorded events centre more on occasional accidents and breakdowns.

Over the Channel on the morning of 7 September 1917, SSZ.14 suffered an engine failure. Despite the mechanic's efforts, his Hawk stayed silent. Drifting on the wind the airship began to sink; her crew jettisoned loose equipment. By 6.30 pm SSZ.14 had wandered 40 miles south of Start Point, Devon. To keep height more items were thrown overboard: the Lewis machine-gun and ammunition trays, revolvers and pyrenes, cartridges and cover for the Aldis lamp, even oil drained from the engine and water from its radiator.

SSZ.14 continued south; around 9.15 pm that evening she floated across the Brittany coast and finally came to earth at St Jean du Doigt near Roscoff, having free-ballooned around 120 miles. Once deflated, the craft was taken by wagon to the French airship station at Guipavas. Its errant engine repaired, two weeks later SSZ.14 flew back to Mullion, no-one the worse for their adventure. The airship's commander, Flight

▲ Mullion, summer 1918: airship SS2.42 gets underway for a patrol. In the gondola, the mechanic stands to tend his Hawk engine (AUTHOR'S COLLECTION).

▲ Wearing an assortment of uniforms, a group of Mullion men gather around an SSZ airship gondola (Ian Stratford).

▲ Rare visitor: airship C*10 over RNAS Bude's lonely mooring-out station, summer 1918. Below, Flight Commander T P York Moore, commander of airship C.9 after Flight Lieutenant Struthers, sends a signal by semaphore flag (author's collection).

Lieutenant Elliott, was later promoted to Captain but his luck didn't improve: later he was in command of C.23a when it came down off Newquay.

Other Mullion Zeros also experienced misfortunes. In strong winds during January 1918 SSZ.25 broke from its moorings and was wrecked. April saw SSZ.15 crash in the sea off Exmouth. SSZ.40 made a forced landing at Leedstown near Camborne on 21 December, but the damaged craft wasn't finally written off until October 1919.

To allow wider airship patrols off Cornwall and south-west England, the Admiralty built several small mooring-out stations in and around the Duchy, bases with only essential facilities. All reported to Mullion, and were commissioned over the spring and summer of 1918. One appeared south of Bude on Cornwall's north-east coast, another outside Plymouth at Laira. Further out-stations were formed at Toller (Bridport, Dorset) and Upton (Poole, Dorset). A site was considered for Scilly at Holy Vale, St Mary's, but wasn't built.

Royal Naval Air Station Bude flew Coastal and SSZ craft. The base was sited two miles south of Marhamchurch and south-east of Langford Wood, roughly equidistant between Langford Hill and Langford Bridge. To help with its construction Mullion personnel travelled up from the Lizard. A clearing was made in a wooded area, creating a natural windbreak for the airships. Bude's officers were billeted at nearby Langford Barton House while the ratings lived on site, in the usual dank bell tents and a few huts; all told, around 200 people. Hydrogen for the airships, contained in high-pressure cylinders, was brought from Mullion's manufacturing plant.

Generally Bude's airships watched over the St George's and Bristol Channels, and west toward the Irish Sea. On station, moored in the open air they were anchored at three points, tied to iron mooring rings set in heavy concrete balls. Like Mullion, Bude was isolated but for off-duty personnel a favourite distraction was the Bullers Arms at nearby Marhamchurch village.

Bude's patrols were usually routine; apart from its usual beat though, airship SSZ.42 flew an unexpected humanitarian mission. One Sunday the craft was abruptly called out to escort two steamers up the Bristol Channel. But on the way, a brief diversionary flight was made allowing crewman Stephen Henry Bromhead to drop a message into his sweetheart's Marhamchurch garden, telling her he'd be late for their date.

▲ Airship C*6 flew from Mullion on convoy protection duties over the summer and autumn of 1918 (TONY MAASZ).

Coastal Star (C*) Class airships also flew from Cornish bases. The earlier Coastal's open gondola layout was kept but the skinning of the C* version was stronger, plywood replacing fabric. To improve the downward view triplex portholes were let into the gondola sides; the floor included a further triplex section, overcoming a blind spot directly below the craft. Larger and more graceful than the Coastal, the envelope of most C* airships was nearly 220 feet long; a rare indulgence too at that time, the five crewmen were allowed parachutes. Though the type was successful, the war's end meant only ten were built.

During the summer and autumn of 1918 two C* airships were based in Cornwall. C*6 arrived at Mullion on 29 May 1918 and stayed until 20 August, when it travelled up-country for major repairs. Mid-October saw a return; it was finally dismantled during March 1919, having flown a total of 522 hours. C*10 served at Mullion, Bude, and latterly Toller where eventually in October 1919 it too was decommissioned.

Cornwall's Own Airship

At Mullion, the engineless cross-Channel wanderings of airship SSZ.14 had caused furrowed brows. The SSZ's Hawk motor was considered generally dependable, while to an extent airship landings without power could be controlled. Over dry land such descents weren't usually fatal, the crew perhaps thrown around on impact but usually more-or-less undamaged. For long maritime patrols though, was it too chancy to rely on just a single engine?

SSZ.14's unplanned voyage gave rise to Cornwall's own airship. The creation of a group led by Flight Lieutenant R L Montagu, early in 1918 a prototype was built in a corner of Mullion's main airship shed. The new craft was christened the Mullion Twin, or MT-1; over the summer she was redesignated SSE.2, the 'E' for Experimental, and also acquired the rather fulsome local name *Silver Queen*.

MT-1 was powered by two Hawks positioned one each side of her stubby gondola, mounted on outriggers and driving pusher propellers. Seating was for four or five: one or two pilots, a wireless operator, coxswain and engineer. Initially given an envelope of 85,000 cubic feet, to improve her performance the volume was increased to 100,000 cu ft, with a length of 165 ft.

Brightening their Monday morning, on 4 March 1918 the whole station turned out to see the Mullion Twin make her maiden flight. MT-1's first ascent lasted just over an hour and test-pilot Montagu achieved a praiseworthy 55 knots. Eleven days later though, attempting to set down during a storm, the new craft crash-landed in Devon's River Plym. Repaired, she continued her testing but crashed a second time though with only slight damage.

Despite her accidents, overall the Mullion Twin's trials were felt successful. MT-1 became the basis of a new airship class, the Submarine Scout Twin. The Admiralty planned to build 115 SSTs by mid-1919, but only 13 had appeared by the time the war ended. Of those, SST.2 served at the RNAS outstation at Toller in Dorset controlled by Mullion, and also visited the parent station.

Meanwhile, Mullion's renamed SSE.2 took part in bomb-dropping tests, using dummy and later real bombs against a circular ground target at the station's southern edge. The resultant craters were sometimes inspected by servicemen, particularly those interested in the Lizard's unusual geology. Her evaluation complete, SSE.2 was then detailed off for secret equipment trials.

▲ RNAS officers and men in front of Mullion's main airship shed, 1918. Flight Lieutenant R L Montagu, the Mullion Twin's designer, is seated to our left. The shed doors were so huge and heavy they were mounted on wheels; often they were moved by traction engines, or teams of horses (AUTHOR'S COLLECTION).

▲ The Mullion Twin's gondola looking forward, with pusher engines installed on their outriggers. For her crew the racket must have been deafening, and there was very little room (AUTHOR'S COLLECTION).

By 1918 a new weapon had emerged in the U-boat war: the acoustic hydrophone. The device was intended to detect submerged submarines by listening for their engine noise. That summer SSE.2 carried out trials code-named *Rubber Eel*, the hydrophone equipment on long leads dangling from her gondola into Mount's Bay, and later the Lizard's less benign waters. Results seemed promising and installation of the system was planned for all SSZs and SSTs. However, the Armistice brought the idea to a close.

The Mullion Twin also saw battle. On 7 September 1918 she helped shepherd the damaged troop-ship *Persic* to St Mary's, part of an air and sea force attending the vessel. In between looking out for U-boats, on the journey she spotted a couple of drifting sea mines, detonated with machine-gun fire.

A month later, during the afternoon of 11 October, Mullion's own airship joined an attack by aircraft and surface vessels on a submarine south of Scilly. In the combined assault numerous bombs and depth charges were dropped; subsequently oil was seen on the surface, suggesting the U-boat had been damaged. This was one of the area's final confrontations.

▲ 4 March 1918: the Mullion Twin being readied for her first flight. Three crewmen are in the gondola; a fourth prepares to fire up the starboard engine while a group holds the craft steady. Officers and men wait for the moment of truth (AUTHOR'S COLLECTION).

▲ Later in life the Mullion Twin was designated SSE.2, as shown on her envelope which also received a silver protective finish. She's seen at her home station, a team manhandling her across the field (AUTHOR'S COLLECTION).

With peace, the Mullion Twin disappeared. We know she was dismantled, and her engines taken away when the RAF left the Lizard. Her gas-bag would have had little value; airship envelopes of the time were fragile, requiring frequent upkeep to prevent leaks and tears. The aluminium and ash gondola was probably scrapped, altogether a sad end for a unique and gallant craft.

Aircraft: Mullion, Padstow, Newlyn, Tresco

From 1 February 1917, Germany had entered a new phase of unrestricted submarine warfare against all merchant vessels found in British and Irish waters. The effect was immediate and devastating. During March, 594,000 tons of merchant shipping was sunk of which 353,000 tons was British; in April a truly appalling 881,000 tons was lost. Thousands of sailors lost their lives, while the onslaught naturally drove off many neutral ships.

Sinkings around the Cornish coast mirrored the wider picture. On 1 February 1917 cargo ship SS *Essonite*, sailing from Caernarfon to Rochester, was sunk by the U-55 (*Kapitänleutnant* Wilhelm Werner) 3 miles NNW of Trevose Head; 10 sailors were lost. That day too, Werner intercepted and scuttled the fishing boat *Ada*, and sank armed smack *Inverlyon* with gunfire. The next day Russian sailing vessel *Pomoschnick* was stopped and scuttled. On 6 February, three miles NNE of Gurnard's Head, U-55 torpedoed petrol-carrier SS *Saxon Briton*, with more loss of life. The following day around 40 miles SW of Scillonia, Werner sank wheat-carrying SS *Yola*, lost with all 33 hands.

As part of the Admiralty's drive to counter the horrendous state of affairs, four additional naval aircraft arrived in Cornwall to augment the aerial anti-submarine patrols. This might seem a paltry gesture, but actually reflected a terrible lack of resources at the time. During their campaign supporting ground forces in France that spring, the British had lost no fewer than 245 aeroplanes together with nearly all their crews.

Mullion

In mid-April four Sopwith 1½ Strutter single-engined biplanes arrived at Mullion, accompanied by Squadron Commander John T Cull DSO and three Flight Sub-Lieutenants. The aircraft came in two versions: two-seat fighters (N5607 and N5608) and single-seat bombers (N5601 and N5602). Use of landplanes was a second choice; the Admiralty would have preferred water-based aircraft but none were available.

A single Bessoneau hangar was erected for the Sopwiths, near the larger airship shed. When not on U-boat patrols, sometimes the two-seaters were used for aerial

▲ Sopwith 1½ Strutter N5624 two-seat fighter at RNAS Mullion, its pilot and observer aboard. Ground crew prepare to start the engine and release the wheel chocks. Behind is a windbreak of the larger airship shed (J M BRUCE/G S LESLIE COLLECTION).

photography; over the summer several more aircraft arrived. By November though only two Sopwiths remained, the rest moved to other duties.

Early the following year their replacements began to appear; de Havilland DH.6 biplanes, simple two-seat aircraft originally designed for pilot training. During May and June 1918, Nos.515 and 516 (Special Duties) Flights were created using the DH.6s. In May too No.493 Flight formed, operating bigger, more substantial de Havilland DH.9 two-seat biplanes; eventually six hangars were provided for Mullion's aircraft. Later, as part of the restructuring of Britain's air services Mullion's three Flights were brought together as No.254 Squadron Royal Air Force. On 20 August that unit was reorganised as No.236 Squadron.

Padstow

Padstow's DH.6 biplanes were as much a burden as a fighting force. The DH.6 was a depressing aeroplane, its engine puny and reticent; many examples also suffered from structural problems. Carrying bombs was a great burden but a load of 100 lb was just about manageable, provided the pilot flew alone. Sometimes DH.6s patrolled merely as unarmed signalling aircraft, the observer using an Aldis lamp to commune with those below.

▲ De Havilland DH.6 C7847 at Mullion, with a group of officers plus four-legged friend, summer 1918. The aircraft flew with Nos.254 and 236 Squadrons (J M BRUCE/G S LESLIE COLLECTION).

Patrols usually lasted around two hours, back and forth over an inshore area say 40 miles across. To help spot the enemy, flights were low-level; in any case the DH.6's ability to climb while lugging bombs was feeble. If aircraft returned to Padstow still carrying their bombload, often they couldn't make enough height to clear the cliffs and reach the landing-ground. That meant a turbulent flight along the nearby valley south of Gunver Head, followed by a drop onto the airfield. Numerous airmen flying from RNAS home stations had previously suffered war injuries deeming them unfit for service overseas, but Padstow's DH.6 patrols would have taxed those in sparkling health.

Meanwhile the base was given a lofty airship mooring mast, ideal where visiting airships were envisaged rather than permanent residents. Padstow occasionally hosted SSZs from Mullion and Bude, particularly if the weather worsened while they were flying locally. Callers soon acquired the shared nickname *The Pig*, conferred by local people – a general moniker since it was tricky to tell them apart.

Many misfortunes befell the DH.6s. On patrol during mid-May 1918, C6678 ran out of fuel and crash-landed in the sea; a passing vessel towed it back to land. It was dried out and re-entered service, but nine days later went missing and was never seen again.

▲ Aerial view of RNAS Padstow/Crugmeer airfield, summer 1918. The three canvas hangars were later joined by a fourth. To their left are lines of bell tents, while 11 DH.6 biplanes rest on the grass; bottom right is the motor transport area. To the left of the station are farm buildings (J M BRUCE/G S LESLIE COLLECTION).

▲ Well-wrapped against the coming cold, a Padstow DH.6 pilot prepares for a patrol. Considering his horrible aeroplane he seems remarkably cheerful (J M BRUCE/G S LESLIE COLLECTION).

▲ De Havilland DH.9 of Padstow's No.494 Flight, summer 1918, armed with underwing bombs. In the background skulks a DH.6 of either No.500 or No.501 Flight (MALCOLM MCCARTHY COLLECTION).

C6683 made a forced landing on 28 May, again in the water; another crashed at the Trethewell estate near St Eval.

On 4 July C5194 also came down in the sea, but was salved by the collier *Brook* and taken to Newlyn, its pilot safe. Just two days later C6682 crashed three miles south of Bude though again, the airman survived. On 23 July C5205 struck C7858 while landing at Padstow, but somehow everyone lived to tell the tale.

Attacks were rare. On 23 July 1918 Captain H Goodfellow, flying No.250 Squadron's C5206, sighted a U-boat 3 miles off Trevose Head and duly dropped a small bomb: no effect. C7849, also of No.250 and piloted by Lieutenant A C Tremellon, bombed a suspected submarine on 27 July. Again, no result. The following month Lieutenant H H Shorter in C5207 spotted a U-boat off Newquay, releasing two bombs; both failed to explode. Ten days later, as if exhausted by its effort, C5207 too came down in the sea. From May 1918 de Havilland DH.9s started to arrive, stronger, more powerful and trustworthier aeroplanes which helped see out Padstow's war.

Newlyn

At Newlyn as elsewhere in Cornwall, patrols were sometimes stopped by the weather but the Short 184 floatplanes flew whenever they could. On 16 March 1917, 8350 bombed a U-boat 10 miles south-south-east of Dodman Point but couldn't confirm a result. Later that month 8049 was safely towed into Falmouth following engine failure over the sea, but was damaged there on 1 April in a freak snowstorm.

During August and September, N1605 and N1604 respectively tackled what they thought were submarines, but both without a conclusive outcome. On 19 December though, 10 miles south-west of the Lizard, N1606 probably damaged a U-boat which had just attacked a convoy. The pilot spotted its torpedo track; bombs were released, air seen rising to the surface.

In February 1918 Newlyn received its first American pilot when Ensign Benjamin Lee, seconded from the US Naval Reserve, made the overnight journey down from Paddington. He was soon in the worst kind of action. On the murky late afternoon of 3 March Lee fired up his Short 184's 240 hp Renault-Mercedes engine; with his British observer, Sub-Lieutenant Bertram Rowley, he began a patrol east of the Lizard. Five minutes into the flight his wireless failed. Constant buffets from a strengthening easterly wind made Lee feel airsick, and it began to grow dark. Compass luminosity was poor; the men became lost.

▲ Short 184 floatplane N2958 seen from the mouth of a Newlyn hangar. Ground crew prepare the aircraft for launching; between its floats, bombs are mounted. In the background is Newlyn's south pier, which for a brief time had two lighthouses (MALCOLM McCARTHY COLLECTION).

▲ Short 184 N1609 '4' came to grief in mid-May 1918, seen nose-down in Mount's Bay as rescuers arrive. The aircraft was safely beached, but scrapped after an inspection (MALCOLM MCCARTHY COLLECTION).

At last, in the deep gloom they spotted a light and settled on the water, but struck a reef; the Short's floats were shattered and it began to sink. Lee had landed by the Eddystone lighthouse, in rough seas. Yet he was blessed that night; keeper Mr Williams heard the commotion, flung him a life-buoy and dragged him through the waves to an iron ladder. Up in the lighthouse the men watched helplessly as Rowley's Aldis lamp chattered from the wrecked aircraft. Finally, it went out. Lee soon returned to duty but his observer was never seen again.

On 24 March 1918, Ensign Lee's new Short broke a con-rod south of Land's End and he ditched once again, that time rescued by a passing trawler. Short N1616 claimed a suspected sinking on 16 May; N2631 and N2958 made separate attacks during 30 June. N1770 bombed an oil slick on 13 July, unsure of its source but determined not to lose a possible opportunity, though the result was doubtful even to the airmen.

Meanwhile, on 1 April 1918 the Royal Air Force had been created, and the Royal Naval Air Service came to an end. The RNAS's South Western Group was disbanded and No.9 (Operations) Group RAF formed at Mount Wise, Devonport, commanding all Cornish air stations – and others – as well as Tresco.

▲ Between October 1918 and January 1919, Short 184 N2988 flew with No.235 Squadron. It's on Newlyn's hard-standing, wearing a simple beaching chassis. The cottage behind the hangar became the officers' day quarters (REG WATKISS COLLECTION).

▲ Newlyn personnel, 1918: Ellis, Henderson, Banks, Graves, Woodland; Ginman, Stanley, Astle, Scott-Evans, Davidson, Harrison, Welbourne, McLeod; Watson, Speight, Lushington, Mills, Callaway, Murray, Hoskins, Terry; Brewer, Blanksby, Nixon, Dunn. The CO, Squadron Commander J S Mills DSC, was well-liked for his attention to business on the station, and his camaraderie in the wardroom where he greatly enjoyed a game of bridge (AUTHOR'S COLLECTION).

Reporting to No.9 (Operations) Group, at Penzance No.71 (Operations) Wing was established to run Mullion, Newlyn, Padstow/Crugmeer and Tresco on a more day-to-day basis. In Penzance too, York House saw a final RNAS shindig as Newlyn's officers held a dinner followed by speeches and toasts; with help from the wardroom's piano and a few bottles, the evening lurched on until the small hours.

From the end of May 1918, Newlyn's aircraft were organised as Nos.424 and 425 Flights nominally with six aircraft each, though always real strengths were lower. On 20 August, No.235 Squadron was formed from those Flights and Short 320 floatplanes began to arrive, a type developed from the 184s.

As well as the Shorts, at least two small Fairey Hamble Baby single-seat floatplanes (N1191 and N1205) flew from Newlyn. Mount's Bay also saw occasional flying-boat visitors from RNAS Tresco, mostly Curtiss H.12s. 8652 had landed with engine trouble on 11 March 1917; in May 8654 arrived in fog; short of fuel, a further caller appeared during June 1918. A Felixstowe F.3 flying-boat too put down that summer, towed across the bay following engine failure and damaged when it was beached.

Tresco

Tresco's operations began in February 1917 using American Curtiss H.12 twin-engined flying-boats. But June saw a serious accident; by the beach, the station's ammunition store exploded. Aircraftmen 2nd Class William Creasy and Charles Ellingworth died, several other men were injured. Over the next few weeks the store was rebuilt and put back into use; the two casualties were laid to rest nearby at St Nicholas church.

During August, airship landing trials began using Mullion's SSZ.14; subsequent visits to Tresco by Cornwall's airships were rare, though Coastal C.9 is known to have called. By August too, patrol patterns had been drawn up for the areas felt under most threat from the U-boats, extending around 80 miles south-west of Scilly.

The following February the island was visited by two of the new Felixstowe F.2A flying-boats, more powerful than the Curtiss types and among the hardest-hitting aircraft of their day. Subsequently F.3 'boats served at Tresco, similar to the F.2A with substantial endurance and bomb load. From the late spring of 1918, four Flights formed at Tresco: Nos.350, 351, 352 and 353, on 31 May, 30 June, 15 September and 30 September respectively. Over that summer eight F.3s arrived; though it was intended to base 12 on the island, that strength was never reached.

▲ RNAS Tresco, summer 1917. The slipway is complete, the main hangar under construction; to its right is the old mill which the station absorbed. The single long dark building by the beach is the ammunition store. On the shoreline is moored a Curtiss H.12 flying-boat, along with a derelict-looking hull probably from another H.12; a second hull sits on the road from the slipway (J M Bruce/G S Leslie collection).

On 20 August No.234 Squadron formed at Tresco, commanded by Robert Maycock who back in 1917 had searched for a suitable spot to build the base. The two Flights existing at the time of the Squadron's formation retained their identities within it, as did Nos.352 and 353 created after the Squadron itself. As well as the other aircraft types, tiny FBA single-engined flying-boats are said to have served in small numbers.

Tresco's aviators engaged the U-boats with varying results. On 27 April 1917, Curtiss H.12 8654 attacked a submarine which chose not to dive but fought back using its deck gun; perhaps it had been damaged in some earlier incident. The Germans' decision to slog it out proved the right one. Fire from the submarine hit and disabled the H.12; unable to release their bombs the crew flew back to Tresco.

During a patrol north of the islands on 27 May, H.12 8656 with Flt Lt John Hoare and Flt Sub Lt William Anderson aboard spotted a surfaced submarine. Flying through defensive fire the H.12 dropped its entire load of four 100 lb bombs, two of which seemed to strike forward of the conning-tower. The U-boat's stern reared out of the water as it plunged below the surface; however, its parting shot had punctured the flying-boat's starboard engine radiator.

In mid-air, taking drastic measures crewman Chief Petty Officer Mechanic John Tadman clambered onto the wing of the H.12. Clinging to the struts around the engine he plugged the hole with rags, holding his improvised bung in place for the 20-minute flight home. At the time it was believed the submarine had been sunk; the crew received medals, including Distinguished Service Crosses for Hoare and Anderson and a Conspicuous Gallantry Medal for Tadman. Only much later did it emerge that actually, the U-boat had survived its ordeal.

Anderson and 8656 made another suspected sighting on 29 May, and again released four bombs. Despite an oily patch which developed on the water though, only a possible sinking was claimed. Four weeks later, on 25 June, H.12 8665 aimed three 100 lb bombs at a U-boat spotted 10 miles north of Cape Cornwall. The submarine had been preparing to attack a hospital ship and though its destruction wasn't confirmed, the aircraft drove it away.

On 21 August 1917, H.12 8680 flown by Flt Lt Hoare dropped three 100 lb bombs at a U-boat 55 miles south-south-west of Scilly. During a patrol on 14 October with Flt Lt F S McGill and Flt Sub Lt Anderson at the controls, the same aircraft attacked

▲ In mid-1918 a Felixstowe F.3 flying-boat from Tresco suffered engine problems and landed in Mount's Bay. RNAS Newlyn personnel hurried to the scene but despite their efforts, during its beaching the aircraft was damaged. Ropes are lashed around its propellers (AUTHOR'S COLLECTION).

▲ RNAS Tresco's shop, under canvas before a wooden building was allocated. Behind its guardian, provisions include biscuits, tobacco, soap and jars of honey (AUTHOR'S COLLECTION).

a submarine caught 15 miles south-west of St Mary's. Four days later, 8656 crewed by McGill, Flt Sub Lt Morgan Smith, Air Mechanic 1(E) Hopkins and AM 2(WT) Newbold unleashed four 100 lb bombs at a U-boat 35 miles south-west of Bishop Rock. Following the strike oil and air bubbles were noticed, thought to be from the damaged submarine.

1918 was equally eventful. During a flight with H.12B N4341 on 10 May, Lt M O Fairhurst attacked and damaged the U-103 with two 230 lb bombs. Two days later, no lesser vessel than the RMS *Olympic* – sister to *Titanic* and by then a camouflaged troopship – finished off the Germans by ramming them.

On 7 September west of Scilly, Capt C R H Stewart flying F.3 N4238 spied the liner *Persic* under U-boat attack. Seeing the aircraft, the submarine dived; Stewart dropped his bombs and by wireless requested surface vessels to tow the damaged *Persic* to St Mary's. H.12B N4341 struck again on 11 October, after a possible U-boat wake was spotted around four miles from incoming transatlantic convoy HH.71. The wake's head was bombed and subsequently oil patches appeared on the water, but it was felt the submarine had managed to slink away.

Paradoxically in terms of their flying, off duty Tresco's airmen experienced the most tranquil of surroundings. The island's population was fewer than 300 souls, and in such a quiet setting most man-made amusements simply didn't exist. But on a fine day the walks, flora and birdlife were beautiful, while sailing trips were arranged to St Mary's and other islands. Shown the ropes by local people, fishing supplemented service fare and the food from Tresco's small shop. Parades took place at St Nicholas church and in summertime the station organised sports days; photographs show competitors enjoying a pleasant smoke between races.

Respite was a blessed relief from the hazards of patrol work. On 11 March 1917, H.12 8652 had to be beached after it began to sink in Mount's Bay; soon afterwards it was scrapped. Caught in a gale on 9 May, H.12 8664 crashed and exploded a mile off tiny Gugh Island, south of Tresco; its crew of Flt Sub Lt Railton, Flt Sub Lt Whigham and Leading Mechanic Birse were killed.

On 5 June, H.12 8654 was forced to put down off Trevose Head; it proved impossible to make a return home by air. Amazingly, in stages the aircraft was towed all the way back to Tresco, though during its journey the wings and tail were damaged. 8654 was repaired, but on 21 July it was struck by 8686 while taking off: another visit to the workshop.

Scilly can experience extreme weather; as the new year of 1918 approached, on 16 December ferocious westerly gales battered the islands. Three H.12s (8665, 8680 and 8686) moored off East Grimsby's beach were wrecked by the winds, parting their cables and tossed around until they broke up; the storm also damaged H.12 8674. During January and February the weather stayed so poor that patrols fell to almost nothing.

By the spring though it was business as usual, and the summer saw more accidents. On 14 June 1918, after landing near Bishop Rock lighthouse with a crankshaft failure, H.12 8675 caught fire and was destroyed; Lt Fairhurst survived but two crewmen were drowned. On 7 August, only 10 days after its arrival at Tresco, F.3 N4000 crashed while taking off in the hands of Flt Sub Lt Anderson. The aircraft bounced across the water until part of its hull gave way; fortunately Anderson managed to beach it on the nearby island of Samson. Later that month, on 22 August N4001 came down near the station; despite attempts to retrieve it the F.3 sank, though its fortunate crew survived.

Compared with Tresco's flying-boats, its Short 184s led quieter lives; that said, they suffered their fair share of engine failures. From time to time the floatplanes were recovered by fishing-boats, naval auxiliaries or the Mount's Bay motor launches; ML319, ML350 and ML359 all gave tows. But on 10 May 1918 in a more serious incident, while returning from a patrol Short 184 N2797 caught fire, the cause a broken petrol pipe. Its crew, Captain C R Morrish DSC and Lieutenant J L Feather, were burned and the aircraft was struck off charge.

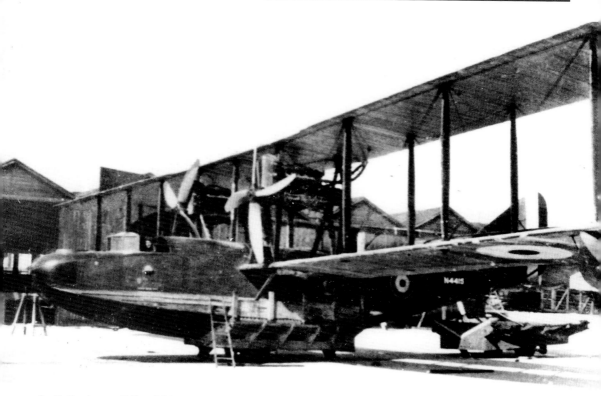

▲ Felixstowe F.3 of No.234 Squadron based at Tresco, caught during the summer of 1918. The slipway is just out of shot to the left; in the background, some of Tresco's workshops (CHRIS ASHWORTH).

On 6 July Short floatplane N2963 failed to return from a patrol. One of the aircraft which went to search, Tresco's F.3 N4234, suffered a petrol leak and was forced to land in heavy seas. Its crew were picked up by a hospital ship, former liner *Braemar Castle*, but under tow the flying-boat sank. Eventually the missing Short was washed up at Audienne in Brittany; Lieutenant Cyril Capes and 2nd Lieutenant James Hendry were buried at Guilvinec, near Quimper.

Long periods moored off New Grimsby didn't help Tresco's aircraft. Water soakage into wooden hulls and floats, and corrosion of metal parts always caused problems. Not the least anxiety was deterioration of bomb-release mechanisms which led them to malfunction. But finally, 10 November 1918 saw the last wartime patrol. During Tresco's short life its most active aeroplane had been H.12B N4341, which arrived in March 1918 and by October had logged almost 240 flying hours.

Chapter 5 - Heroes

I**T MIGHT BE** said anyone who endured the anguish of the First World War was a hero, whether in the trenches, at sea, or high in the air. Here are some men and women of Cornish association whose particularly valiant stories have come down to us.

Horace Curtis

Horace Augustus Curtis was born in 1891 at St Anthony on the Roseland, but grew up near Newlyn East. As a boy he excelled at cross-country running and won many races for Cornwall. On leaving school he became a china-clay worker but when war began volunteered for the DCLI; quickly though he was transferred to the Royal Dublin Fusiliers.

For four years Horace fought constantly, at Gallipoli in Turkey, Greece and Palestine, and was promoted to Sergeant. Over the summer of 1918 he was granted 10 days' home leave; it was his first since the outbreak. In September he was posted to France and by the following month was fighting at Le Cateau in the north-east, where a savage battle broke out.

▶ In October 1918 Horace Curtis was awarded the Victoria Cross, following his heroism on the Western Front (AUTHOR'S COLLECTION).

Attacking, his platoon came under heavy fire. To avoid the assault failing Horace charged, alone. In a moment he'd killed or wounded two German machine-gun teams; four more surrendered. Still unaided, this courageous soldier then captured a whole trainload of stunned enemy troops meant as reinforcements. Finally his men caught up with him and Horace handed over his prisoners; he was uninjured.

For his gallantry, at Buckingham Palace Sergeant Curtis received the Victoria Cross from King George V, the only Cornishman fighting on the Western Front to whom it was awarded. Horace rarely spoke of his medal, humbled that he'd been recognised while many of his friends hadn't survived the war. He enjoyed a long life in Cornwall, and died at Redruth in 1968.

Theodora Fox Harvey

In August 1914 Miss Helen Theodora Fox Harvey, who lived in the Probus area, joined the Queen Alexandra's Royal Naval Nursing Service Reserve. Born in 1883, we may suppose she came from a medical background; the Reserve had been created during 1910 by civilian hospitals which agreed to supply nurses at short notice if war broke out.

A few weeks after she'd volunteered Theodora's life was transformed; she embarked in the old pre-Dreadnought battleship HMS *Albion*, by then a hospital ship. On board she made many friends, one four-legged: the ship's terrier, Buller. By July 1915 her work had taken her to the white-painted hospital Mission steamer *Queen Alexandra*, at first sailing in the grey North Sea.

For her duties, Theodora wore a white handkerchief cap with a naval crown embroidered in one corner, together with a navy-blue linen dress with red cuffs, and a blue tippet bearing the Red Cross emblem. Nurses were treated as officers and Theodora was addressed as Madam. For a time she worked just off the French coast near Dunkirk, helping with wounded men while German forces shelled the town; subsequently *Queen Alexandra* was based at Dover.

Theodora rose to become a Nursing Sister. She continued to serve her country throughout the war and after a long life, died in 1970. Today her war work is recognised on a plaque in Probus parish church.

Thomas Rendle

Among the first troops to arrive in France during August 1914, 1st Battalion, the Duke of Cornwall's Light Infantry numbered within its ranks Bandsman Thomas Edward Rendle. Born in 1884 Thomas had joined the regiment during 1912; at the front, like other DCLI bandsmen he became a stretcher-bearer. His battalion was involved in heavy, almost continuous fighting and by November he found himself in Flanders, at the small Belgian border town of Wulverghem.

On the morning of 20 November, German forces began a heavy howitzer bombardment of the DCLI's trenches. Thomas was helping wounded troops when one of the parapets was hit and collapsed, burying a dozen or more men. Speed was everything; Thomas ran to the scene. With bare hands he tore at the soil for his comrades. All the while he was exposed, the flattened earthworks giving no protection as enemy fire zeroed in.

At last though, Thomas had pulled every man out. He crawled back across open ground, carrying badly-wounded 2nd Lieutenant Colebrooke on his back, in full view of the Germans. Finally he returned to the injured soldiers he'd rescued; drained by his effort, he comforted them as best he could until help arrived.

For his "conspicuous bravery" Bandsman Rendle was awarded the Victoria Cross. He was deeply modest; interviewed later by a newspaper he said simply: "There's really nothing in it." During the First World War Thomas was the only DCLI soldier to win the VC. He was also awarded the Russian Order of St George.

▶ Bandsman Thomas Rendle received the DCLI's only Victoria Cross of the First World War (AUTHOR'S COLLECTION).

Shortly after his feat, Thomas suffered injuries to his eyesight from shell bombardment. Sent to Exeter's Eye Infirmary near his wife and children, his convalescence during early 1915 included time at Redruth. He recovered, returned to France, and ended his military career as the 1st Battalion's Band Sergeant. In 1920 he emigrated to South Africa and a new start; he was the only one of six brothers to survive the war. Today, Thomas Rendle's Victoria Cross is kept at the Duke of Cornwall's Light Infantry Museum in Bodmin.

Cora Ball

▲ Young Truro woman Cora Cornish Ball, who went to France to serve her country (AUTHOR'S COLLECTION).

Truro's war memorial on Boscawen Street honours just one woman from the First World War: deceptively delicate-looking Cora Cornish Ball. Born in 1896 to a large family, for a time Cora lived in Kenwyn village near the city. Her father had various jobs and the family moved around the local area. Despite that, Cora kept up her schooling until she was 14 or so, and in 1917 the slim young girl volunteered for service with the Women's Army Auxiliary Corps.

As Corps No.2717, Cora travelled to France where she served near Calais. Her WAAC uniform consisted of a khaki cap atop her short dark bob, with a matching khaki jacket and skirt; regulations stipulated the skirt must be no more than 12 inches above the ground. During her war service, perhaps because she'd stayed on at school Cora reached the rank of Forewoman, equivalent to an army sergeant.

The WAAC was formed in 1917; it provided storekeeping, vehicle maintenance and clerical duties for the British Army, as well as telephonists, waitresses and cooks, freeing more men to take up fighting roles. In the following year the WAAC was renamed

Queen Mary's Army Auxiliary Corps; between January 1917 and November 1918 more than 57,000 women enlisted.

Cora received two medals recognising her war service: the Victory Medal, and the British War Medal. Sadly though, only 11 days following the Armistice she died, perhaps a victim of the terrible flu pandemic sweeping Europe at the time. Cora Ball was laid to rest in Les Baraques Military Cemetery at Sangatte, near Calais; she was just 22.

Cora's name appears in a 1920s manuscript titled *British Women's Work During the Great War*, held by London's Imperial War Museum, which includes rolls of honour recording the hundreds of British nurses and servicewomen who gave their lives on active service. Today, as well as being remembered by Truro's monument Cora Ball is honoured on the memorial in her home village.

Ernest Pitcher

In July 1903, at just 15 years old, Ernest Herbert Pitcher joined the Royal Navy. Born at Mullion on New Year's Eve 1888, father George worked as a coastguard and by August 1914 Ernest was serving in the Dreadnought battleship *King George V*. The following year he volunteered for special service with Britain's growing Q-ship fleet.

Q-ships were intended to combat Germany's submarines by posing as defenceless merchant vessels. To inflict a nasty surprise on attacking U-boats these tempting targets

▶ In 1917 Mullion's heroic seaman Ernest Pitcher was awarded the Victoria Cross (AUTHOR'S COLLECTION).

concealed weaponry aplenty: deck-guns, torpedoes, depth-charges. It was perilous work, the Q-ships serving as decoys to draw enemy fire, their crews all volunteers.

In February 1917, ex-collier Q-ship HMS *Farnborough* was sailing off Ireland's west coast. Among her crew was Ernest, by then a Petty Officer. *Farnborough* was attacked by submarine U-83; in a brutal exchange the U-boat was sunk, the ship damaged but beached, while Ernest was mentioned in despatches.

By the summer he was embarked in HMS *Dunraven*, again a Q-ship disguised as a collier. On 8 August, around 130 miles south-west of Ushant in the Bay of Biscay, submarine UC-71 spotted *Dunraven*. Taken in, the U-boat surfaced and attacked. Shells from its deck-gun struck the ship, setting off depth-charges; fire caught at her stern while a torpedo caused more damage.

The British replied with two torpedoes of their own, but missed. UC-71 stole away while *Dunraven* slowly began to go down; later she sank under tow. Happily the crewmen who'd lived through the action were rescued, and the story of PO Pitcher's gallantry came out.

Ernest had been in charge of the sailors manning *Dunraven*'s 4-inch gun, hidden in the poop. When the magazine below was set afire, to stave off catastrophe the men carried all the powder and shells they could up to their gun. There they calmly held these materials on their knees, to stop the deck's heat igniting them. Finally though the magazine had exploded; the sailors were blown high into the air. With several injuries, Ernest came round on the deck.

Somehow, all the gun-crew had survived. In the light of such exceptional discipline and bravery, along with the other sailors Ernest's name was entered into a ballot for a Victoria Cross, and drawn. He received his medal in November 1917; his men were awarded Conspicuous Gallantry Medals.

In July 1918 Petty Officer Pitcher VC and his wife Lily attended a private view of the Exhibition of Naval Photographs at the Princes Galleries in Piccadilly, London, where they met King George V and Queen Mary. After the war, as a regular Ernest stayed in the Navy; during August 1920 he was promoted to Chief Petty Officer, and that year was a member of the honour guard at the Cenotaph Service of Remembrance. He left the Service in 1927, becoming a teacher and then a publican. During August 1940, at the height of the Battle of Britain, he rejoined the Navy. Courageous Ernest Pitcher saw out his second great war, and died in February 1946.

Louisa McGrigor

At Newlyn today, on the hill overlooking the harbour is an elegant memorial to Louisa McGrigor. Its panelled inscription tells us she was Commandant of the Cornwall 22 Voluntary Aid Detachment, giving nursing care to war-wounded troops sent to the area. Local Red Cross Workers, the Women's Unionist Association, Boy Scouts, Girl Guides and friends clubbed together to erect the granite monument to Miss McGrigor "in loving memory."

Louisa lived at Newlyn, near Paul Hill; she came from a military family and before the war had been involved with the village's Red Cross work. A cheerful and generous woman, during the war years she toiled to help establish and run the Penzance Voluntary Aid Detachment hospital for wounded servicemen, situated in Morrab Road. As war dragged on, the hospital became ever busier.

▲ The memorial to Louisa McGrigor, set high on the hill overlooking Newlyn's harbour.

Somehow Louisa also found time to create and help run local groups of Sea Scouts and Girl Guides, while on the so-called day of rest she taught at St Peter's Church Sunday School, near her home. Perhaps such overwork affected her health; from nowhere, in March 1917 she developed appendicitis and was taken to the West Cornwall Hospital at Penzance. On 31 March she died, mourned and admired by her community.

It's a measure of the respect in which Louisa was held that her remembrance service at St Mary's Church Penzance was attended by members of the prominent local Bolitho family, representatives from Newlyn's naval and air bases, 22 VAD nursing staff and those patients able to make the short journey, as well as her many friends and acquaintances. Her memorial was unveiled in 1921. Like Cora Ball, she appears in the roll of honour recorded in *British Women's Work During the Great War*. Today, few know of Louisa's wartime work; outside the area she's an unsung hero, but locally her memory's maintained by the fine monument.

John French

Today's Old Cornwall Society is a broad group of local history enthusiasts, with branches across Cornwall. Just outside Redruth the Society runs an excellent museum; among its most prized artefacts is the diary of Sapper John French.

John was a tin miner, born at Redruth in 1892 and one of 11 children. A volunteer soldier, early during 1915 he travelled to France with the 254th Tunnelling Company, Royal Engineers. For two years he kept a detailed diary of life in the trenches, three volumes of immaculate pencilled hand-writing recording his experiences. Many events were shocking: facing gas attacks; digging trenches so near the Germans he could hear their shouted insults; carrying away the dead. In March 1915 he wrote: "There is a pretty smart German sniper and he has killed a number of our men."

▲ John French, the Redruth sapper who kept a diary of life on the Western Front (AUTHOR'S COLLECTION).

But several entries include unexpected flashes of humour. In a "rather curious" episode, during a respite in the fighting a British soldier yelled an invitation across no-man's land to "come on over, Fritz," in a mock-German accent. A Teutonic shout replied in accented English: "No blooming fear." Sometimes, to act as warnings of approaching gas the troops carried caged mice, but in June 1916 the diary recorded: "We got enough gas to make us sick but the mouse was still alive and kicking."

Despite his experiences, it seems John somehow stayed unruffled. He wrote of how war was "rather exciting" and "you never know what's coming next." He rose to Sergeant and later received a field commission as a 2nd Lieutenant. In the latter half of 1917 John fought at Passchendaele and was awarded the Military Cross for "conspicuous bravery."

Though he was injured he survived the war, and during June 1919 returned to Cornwall. He didn't stay long but sailed for America, where he met and married a pianist named Eve. Unhappily though, he developed tuberculosis; aged just 37, John died in 1929. For many years the diary remained lost, but in 2009 was discovered among his late sister's effects. The record is a rare first-hand account reflecting great bravery and fortitude, and today we're privileged to have it safely preserved near John French's home town.

James Finn

James Henry Finn was born in 1893 at St Clement near Truro; he had ten brothers and sisters. The family moved to Bodmin and settled in Downing Street, but when James left school he travelled to the South Wales valleys, looking for work. He found a job at a colliery but when war began enlisted as a medic with his local regiment, the South Wales Borderers, joining the 4th Battalion.

James served at Gallipoli, but by spring 1916 his battalion had moved to Mesopotamia (now Iraq) and was fighting Turkish forces at the First Battle of Kut. On 9 April, south-east of Baghdad at Sannaiyat, the enemy mounted a night attack and many British soldiers were injured. Under heavy fire James crawled into no-man's land, close to the Turks' trenches, to rescue wounded comrades. In separate journeys he carried two men back to his lines, and several times returned to bandage and comfort others. He came under repeated fire and eventually was hit, though he made a recovery.

For his gallantry that night, James was awarded the Victoria Cross; he also received the Order of Karageorge 1st Class, the equivalent medal of Serbia. During the following March though, near Baghdad the heroic Cornishman was wounded again. He was picked up, but his ambulance was hit by enemy fire and Private Finn died; he was just 23 years old. Today he's still remembered on Iraq's Basra Memorial, set amidst a former battle-ground from the first Gulf War.

▲ Cornishman James Finn received the Victoria Cross following his bravery in Mesopotamia. In this doctored image from the time, he's shown with his medal; in real life he never had the chance to wear it (AUTHOR'S COLLECTION).

Chapter 6 - Aftermath

ON 11 NOVEMBER 1918 the Armistice was signed; finally, the terrible all-consuming war ended. In Cornwall, hooters blasted from factories, foundries and mines while harbours and ports resounded to ships' whistles. Church bells rang out, spontaneous services of thanksgiving were held. Hatless, flag-waving crowds gathered in Truro where shops and businesses shut for the day; the revelry and celebrations were echoed across the Duchy. But quite unlike their bull-roaring headlines of August 1914, Cornish newspapers reported Germany's defeat in a sombre tone. The *West Briton* settled for 'End of the War', the *Cornishman* led simply with 'Peace, November 11, 1918', while the *Packet* headline was a plain 'Germany Surrenders'.

Meanwhile, civic festivities and processions were hurriedly organised. Many of the men who'd played in Cornwall's famed brass bands had joined up, so local Boys' Brigades and scouts were drafted to provide the music. Entertainments included public teas with free entry for service people, children's treats advertised as 'tea, races and singing' (hopefully not in that order), firework displays and not least, gleeful burning of Kaiser effigies. However, typical of continuing events for good causes, 21 November saw a fundraising concert at Launceston Town Hall in aid of injured ex-servicemen, put on by the Bude Concert Party; that night the participants and audience must have raised the roof.

Once U-boat commanders at sea had been made aware of the ceasefire, regular airship patrols from Cornwall ended. Occasional missions were still flown, usually to find and destroy left-over mines. But Mullion's base had been a wartime measure, and during 1919 the aviators left as swiftly as they'd arrived. Fittingly the Mullion Twin carried out the station's last airship flight, on 25 January 1919. Those airships which had survived the war were disposed of, and during the summer the site was abandoned; Bude's outstation too was quickly dismantled.

The RAF's aircraft presence in Cornwall also dwindled. In February 1919 Newlyn closed, and No.235 Squadron disbanded during the same month. Padstow/Crugmeer also shut down; its airship mooring-mast was acquired for scrap by Mr Richard Parkyn Snr, landlord of the Farmer's Arms public house at St Merryn. Over the summer of 1919, No.9 (Operations) Group and No.71 (Operations) Wing were dissolved.

▲ Victory parade along Penzance's Alverton Street, November 1918; among the crowd are nurses, the Royal Navy and civic dignitaries (AUTHOR'S COLLECTION).

Command of Tresco's No.234 Squadron had passed to Major G H Cox during the new year. But in mid-May No.234 disbanded, its aircraft and personnel left Tresco and the station closed. The RAF removed valuable items from the site but some buildings remained, starting new lives as bulb sheds for the island's flower traders.

The Duke of Cornwall's Light Infantry had fought around the globe: Aden, Belgium, Bulgaria, Egypt, France, Greece, Italy, India, Palestine, Serbia. Its Territorial battalions had grown and sub-divided, Service battalions too had multiplied; from 1916 conscripts were added. During the war the regiment had raised 15 battalions including Territorial and New Army units, and an additional battalion quickly absorbed by the Somerset Light Infantry. Of the men though, 4,282 had been killed; thousands more were wounded.

▲ On St Mary's, spontaneous celebrations broke out as local people rejoiced at news of the Armistice (AUTHOR'S COLLECTION).

Back in October 1915, 2nd Battalion DCLI had travelled to the rocky landscape of Salonika in Greece where they stayed for the duration. Their fighting had ended six weeks before the wider Armistice, with the Bulgarian opposition's surrender. After the war the DCLI swiftly reverted to its pre-war form, though with a single Territorial battalion rather than two.

◄ Once the RAF had left Mullion its vacant buildings declined. Here, it's the 1920s; a little girl tries her hand at opening the old airship shed's gigantic door while mother has her picture taken (W S TREVENA, VIA PADDY BRADLEY).

▲ At the outbreak of war Lanhydrock's Tommy Agar-Robartes joined the Royal Bucks Hussars and later fought with the Coldstream Guards. Today he's commemorated in Truro Cathedral (AUTHOR'S COLLECTION).

▲ Armistice: alongside Newlyn harbour's North Pier the Royal Navy's MLs are at rest, festooned in bunting. Navy and civilians celebrate, perhaps a family group (MALCOLM MCCARTHY COLLECTION).

Of the young men who'd joined the army from Cornwall's prominent homes, Trengwainton's Edward Bolitho had been mentioned in despatches three times and had twice been wounded, but returned safely. By then he'd received the Military Cross and the Distinguished Service Order. But in September 1915 during the Battle of Loos, Captain Tommy Agar-Robartes had been killed rescuing an injured comrade; popular with Lanhydrock's workers, he was sorely missed. Near Mevagissey, 22 gardening staff from Heligan House had volunteered early in the war; just six came home.

On 11 November 1918 the Navy's Newlyn motor launches stayed silent, their crews joining the delirious celebrations. At Penzance's south dock head, as the Armistice came into force at 11 o'clock the town's RNR commanding officer, by then (Acting) Commander Blair, launched a celebratory rocket. David Blair had made many friends during his four years' service at Penzance and in his spare time was well-known for performing comical songs. He had good reason to be a cheerful soul, having been listed in 1912 for service on the *Titanic*; at the last minute he'd been bumped.

Early in the new year, on Saturday 4 January, out of the rain a forbidding grey shape appeared at Penzance harbour mouth: a U-boat, but defeated, flying the White Ensign. MLs were among the escorting craft, whistles cutting through the winter air as people flocked to the waterfront. U-101 tied up, and over the next few days hundreds inspected the beaten foe; she'd also visited Falmouth. The submarine was later scrapped by J H Slade, Penzance engineers and shipbreakers, whose premises were in Wharf Road.

Like Penzance, over the war Scilly's naval presence had increased: auxiliary vessels included trawlers *Cambria, City of Edinburgh, Foss, Hercules IV, Imelda, Isaac Chant, Nancy Hague, Raindrop, Saurian, Thomas Graham, Thomas Hankins* and *Whitefriars*; drifters *Laurel III, Marvellous* and *Rambling Rose*; and tugs *Blazer, Bramley Moore, Cynic, Epic, Resolve, Revenger* and *Woonda*. But over the weeks following the Armistice the Navy withdrew from Scilly and Cornwall.

The duration officers and men of the RNVR and RNR went back to their former peace-time activities; in March 1919 Holman's dock, vacated, took up its pre-war work. Meanwhile, from around the world thousands of Cornish mariners serving overseas finally came home. Merchant sailor Gordon Roberts from the Lizard's Church Cove had

◀ This 3-pounder deck-gun shell-case was presented by (Acting) Commander David Blair, commanding Penzance's naval force, to C M Mitchell, a Missions to Seamen volunteer, for his wartime work in the town (ALASTAIR COX).

▲ Captured German submarine U-101 in Penzance harbour, opened for public viewing. Admission was 1/6d (7½p) but free to service people (MALCOLM MCCARTHY COLLECTION).

spent the entire war shut up in the Black Sea, where he'd fished to help provide food for the Forces. When he eventually returned to Cornwall he found many of his village friends had died.

By November 1918, the Royal Naval Reserve Trawler Section had grown from 1,200 men and 150 boats to a force of 39,000 men with more than 700 vessels, at home and abroad. After the Armistice though, the Trawler Section was quickly demobilised. Many of the remaining Cornish craft still in reasonable condition were stripped of naval equipment and returned to fishing. Others, worn-out, were scrapped. But for another year or so some converted minesweepers continued their toil, sweeping for the war's leftover mines.

Falmouth too watched the Royal Navy leave, but that wasn't quite the end of the story. In 1921 eight surrendered U-boats appeared, brought by the Navy for trials. Six moored at Gyllyngvase, but during a winter storm five were driven onto the Pendennis rocks. Abandoned, they became a tourist hit. The submarines stayed until the Second World War when with grim irony, they were partly dismantled during Britain's push for scrap-metal. Today the bare bones are still there.

On the home front Cornwall's mining industry, which during the war had undergone a mini-revival, collapsed; by 1921 ore prices had plummeted compared with wartime levels. Fishing too faltered; rebuilding the fleets was difficult due to the initial shortage of good boats and also because sadly, many of the naval reserve lads hadn't returned. But after a slow start, the fishing industry began a recovery.

Within weeks of the Armistice many government contracts for war equipment and materials were cancelled, and Cornish companies fought to recover previous peacetime business. In the face of local mine closures Holmans of Camborne struggled at first, but managed to pull through the slump. By 1920 though, the explosives factories at Hayle, Perranporth and Trago Mills had shut their books; the workers were laid off.

▲ Bodmin, July 1924: outside the barracks, the Prince of Wales attends the dedication of Bodmin's DCLI memorial to those who fell during the First World War. Today the monument is still beautifully cared for (AUTHOR'S COLLECTION).

Truro's Auxiliary Naval Hospital had grown to 210 beds and during its short lifetime treated over 4,000 patients. In March 1919 the Red Cross handed back the buildings to the workhouse board of guardians and the site reverted to its former role. During 1916, Heligan House had been requisitioned by the War Department, becoming an officers' convalescent home until the Tremayne family returned in peacetime. At Cotehele House near Saltash, Lord Mount Edgcumbe allowed servicemen back from the fighting to use portions of his land for market gardening.

As the military left Cornwall, so too did refugees from overseas who'd sought sanctuary from their invaded countries. During March 1919 Madame Alise Roelandt, a Belgian lady, returned to her bloodied homeland. Husband Théophile had died at the siege of Namur, just after the outbreak; she'd arrived at Ladock in January 1915 with her children Hortense, Léon and Stanislas. Before she left, Mme Roelandt presented the parish church with an illuminated inscription acknowledging her gratitude for the kindness of local people. It's still on display there today.

On 11 November 1919 the first Armistice Day was observed. Before 11.00 am Cornish church bells tolled; two minutes' silence followed. Bare-headed and bowed, in towns and villages people stood silently before fresh memorials to the dead.

One small community, though, was unique in Cornwall. The parish of Herodsfoot nestles in the West Looe valley near Liskeard; today it's a gentle place surrounded by woodland. Set on the green, the village's most poignant feature is its granite First World War memorial. For the monument's inscription is truly remarkable; it tells us that during the conflict, Herodsfoot was spared military fatalities.

All 13 of the village men who joined the armed forces came home safely. The memorial records their names, and the parish's "gratitude for their services in the Great War." The handful of British communities which lost no men at all during the First World War have since become known as Thankful Villages; Herodsfoot is Cornwall's only Thankful Village, one of around just 50 across the entire country.

▲ Herodsfoot village's First World War memorial is the only one of its kind in Cornwall (AUTHOR'S COLLECTION).

Chapter 7 - Then and Now

TODAY, THERE'S LITTLE evidence of Cornwall's first aerial bases. Though Padstow/Crugmeer's old airfield is still an open space, no sign survives of its previous use. A grey block-built wireless station is across the lane, but was put up during the Second World War. At Newlyn even the profile of the former aircraft apron has changed, as shoreline spoil from nearby Gwavas quarry has shifted over the years. But Newlyn's south pier is very much in place so it's easy to find the spot.

The airship station at Cury, its land now occupied by wind-farm turbines, has more to see. Both airship shed floors survive, huge flat rectangular surfaces amid the grassland. Massive concrete anchor blocks which once supported the shed entrance windbreaks also remain. Nearby, Cury village hall at White Cross was once an RNAS Mullion

▲ Bodmin's former DCLI barracks at The Keep is now a museum recording the Regiment's history and campaigns. Also on view is a magnificent armoury (OLAF TAUSCH).

▲ On St Mary's many old fortifications survive, including this gun position. You can see
them during a day's stroll around the island; out across the water, the views are beautiful
(AUTHOR'S COLLECTION).

▲ When Tommy comes marching home … the bronze representation of a First World War
Cornish soldier atop Truro's memorial in Boscawen Street. Below are commemorated
the city's war dead: 181 men and one woman (AUTHOR'S COLLECTION).

building, probably the canteen; after the war it was liberated by local people and still puts in good service for the community.

At Tresco too, reminders linger. The stone mill and power house around which the air station was built, its big chimney featured in photographs then and now, offers holiday accommodation. Re-skimmed, the aircraft slipway is used for small boats while the former ammunition store has been converted into three peaceful holiday cottages. Old concrete bases for airmen's huts provide storage areas, and in one case an improvised basketball court. New Grimsby's summer outlooks are still a wide white beach, boats rocking, islands and tiny outcrops scattered across a blue twinkly sea; views almost unchanged from those seen by Tresco's aviators almost a hundred years ago.

As for signs of the army, the former Duke of Cornwall's Light Infantry headquarters at Bodmin is now an impressive military museum, while Pendennis and St Mawes castles have become visitor attractions. On the Roseland at St Anthony's Head, the old gun emplacements and eerie underground magazine survive. Scraesdon Fort is used for military instruction; its maze of rooms and passages are ideal for training soldiers to operate in a built environment. Tregantle houses visiting troops.

These days too, several of Cornwall's Victorian forts are employed peacefully. To the eastern side of Whitsand Bay, Polhawn Fort has become a wedding venue while nearby, part of Cawsands battery is residential and neighbour Hawkins Battery trades as a holiday park. Picklecombe Fort has been converted to apartments. Across the water to the west, on St Mary's much of the Garrison's structure survives; since the 1930s its principal feature, Star Castle, has been a hotel.

⤛ ⋎ ⤜

It's hard, perhaps impossible for us to imagine the innermost thoughts of people who lived and fought during the First World War. But perhaps a word of reflection on those four shattering years can be left to Private Harry Patch.

Harry was Britain's last surviving soldier who'd served in the trenches, and lived until his 112th year. The Duke of Cornwall's Light Infantryman was conscripted in 1916 and fought at Passchendaele's dreadful battle; nearly a hundred years later, his medals are displayed at the DCLI Museum. Today Harry's thoughts ring out: "When the war ended, I don't know if I was more relieved that we'd won or that I didn't have to go back. All those lives lost, for a war finished over a table. Now what's the sense in that?"

Acknowledgements

I'd like to record my grateful thanks to the following people and institutions, for their kind help and support in connection with this book:

Chris Ashworth, John Bennett, Paddy Bradley, Ivan and Heather Corbett, Alastair Cox, Deborah Cuthbert, Gordie Hollow, Mike Ingham, Steve Johnson (Steve's heritage website is Cyberheritage: www.cyber-heritage.co.uk/), G Stuart Leslie, Tony Maasz, Lynne Mayers, Ces Mowthorpe, Don Perry, Bryan Ribbans (Bryan's flying-boat website is Seawings: www.seawings.co.uk), Joy Shellard, Gordon Smith (Gordon's website is www.naval-history.net), Ian Stratford, Derek Tait, Olaf Tausch, W S Trevena, Reg Watkiss, Alix Wood, Cornish Studies Library Redruth, Cornwall At War Museum Davidstow, Fleet Air Arm Museum Yeovilton, Helston Museum, Morrab Library Penzance, Old Cornwall Society, Royal Cornwall Museum Truro.

Special thanks to Malcolm McCarthy for use of images from his collection. Malcolm's website of Cornish records, the Malcolm McCarthy Document Collection, is www.mccarthyindex.org. Over the years he's helped me on numerous projects, with unfailing generosity; this time he's surpassed himself. Many thanks, Malc.

▼ Padstow's Territorial soldiers; seemingly on fatigues, the men are tooled up with a selection of brooms, spades and forks. To the right are their sergeants (MALCOLM McCARTHY COLLECTION).